Mathematical Graphs with GeoGebra

Dibyajyoti Hazarika

June 13, 2024

Dedicated to My Beloved Mother
Late Mrs Subarna Hazarika

Acknowledgement

At the outset, I would like to mention my family-my parents (Late Mrs Subarna Hazarika & Mr Abani Kumar Hazarika), my brother (Purbajyoti) and my sister (Snehajyoti) for there constant inspiration throughout my life. This book is an outcome of my teaching preparation for honours practical classes in Diphu Government College. During preparation of geogebra classes I lost my mother. My mother had always taught me to face challenges and struggles of life with courage, faith and patience. Here, I would like to thanks my students, as it is there curiosity and mistakes in plotting the graphs which make me to learn about the core concepts of the subject.

Next, I would like to thanks Diphu Government College fraternity for providing there support to perform my duties. Special, thanks to my colleagues at Department of Mathematics, Diphu Government College for their support and encouragement at every point of service, since my joining.

Finally, I would like to give thanks to everyone who have helped me directly or indirectly in the preparation of this book, at the same time i would like to express my apology for not mentioning them personally by there names.

Date: (Dibyajyoti Hazarika)
Place:

Contents

List of Figures

Chapter 1

Graphs of Some Simple Functions

In this chapter, we plot the graphs of functions $e^{ax}+b$, $\log(ax+b)$, $1/(ax+b)$, $\sin(ax+b)$, $\cos(ax+b)$, $|ax+b|$ and illustrated the effect of a and b on the graph.

1.1 Graph of function $e^{ax}+b$ and illustrate the effect of a and b on the graph

System requirement:-(i) Windows OS or Android Phone

(ii) Geogebra software

Prerequisite:

(i) Geogebra interface: How to use geogebra

(ii) Knowledge of exponential function.

Exponential Function

The function $y = e^{ax} + b$ is translation of the function $y = e^{ax}$ with the value b. Expansion of function is

$$y = b + (1 + ax + \frac{a^2x^2}{2!} + \frac{a^3x^3}{3!} + ...)$$

The function $y = e^{ax} + b$ is a real valued function defined for all $x \in R$ (set of real number).

Procedure or Geogebra applets for plotting $y = e^{ax} + b$

Step 1: Open geogebra classic 6 on your system.

Step 2: In the input bar, type $a = 1$ then slider for 'a' come. Default value of 'a' varies from -5 to 5.

To change default value to some specified value click on three dots in right hand side in the input bar where $a = 1$ is written then click on setting, go to slider (in geogebra classis 5 this option is not available) and change default value to the specified value.

Step 3: Again, type $b = 1$ then another slider for 'b' will came. The value of 'b' varies from -5 to 5.

Step 4: Next type the function $y = e^{ax} + b$.

Step 5: By changing the position of a and b in the slider. We can see the effect of a and b on the graph.

Observations

1. The graph of $y = e^{ax} + b$ move upward.

2. If $a < b$, $a\,\&\,b$ both are negative then the graph of the function lies below the x-axes and flatter toward right; and move upward toward positive y axes along left side.

3. If $a < b$, $a\,\&\,b$ both are positive then the graph of the function is flatter toward negative x-axes along left; and move upward toward positive y axes along right side.

4. If $a > b$, both $a\,\&\,b$ are negative then the graph of the function lies below the x-axes and flatter toward right; and move upward toward positive y axes along left side.

5. If $a > b$, both $a\,\&\,b$ are positive then left hand side of the graph is flatter and

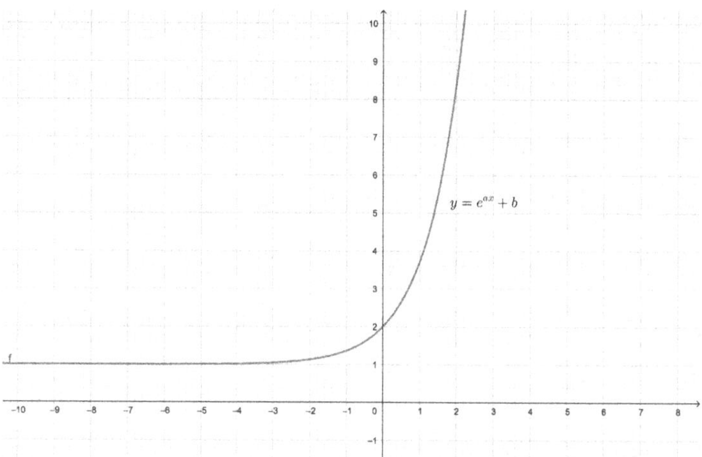

Figure 1.1: Graph of the function $y = e^{ax} + b$

lies below x-axes and right side move upward toward positive y-axes.

6. If $a = b = 0$, the curve is a straight line parallel to x-axes through the line $y = 1$

Conclusion

The graph of the function $y = e^{ax} + b$ is obtained as shown in figure 1.1.

1.2 Graph of the function $\log(ax + b)$ and effect of a and b on the graph

System requirement:- (i) Windows OS or Android Phone

(ii) Geogebra software.

Prerequisite: (i) Geogebra interface: How to use geogebra

(ii) Knowledge of logarithm.

Logarithm

The basic logarithm function is the function $y = \log_b x$ where $y, b > 0$ and $b \neq 1$. When no base is mention we take the base 10.

The domain is the set of all positive real number.

Expansion of logarithm function is

$$\log(1 + x) = x - \frac{x^2}{2} + \frac{x^3}{3} - \frac{x^4}{4} + \frac{x^5}{5} - \dots$$

provided x is real and $|x| < 1$

$\log(b+ax) = \log(b(1+\frac{ax}{b}))$ [using properties of logarithm $\log(a.b) = \log a + \log b$]

$= \log b + \log(1 + \frac{ax}{b})$

$= \log b + \frac{ax}{b} - \frac{a^2 x^2}{2b^2} + \frac{a^3 x^3}{3b^3} - \frac{a^4 x^4}{4b^4} + \frac{a^5 x^5}{5b^5} - \dots$

provided $|\frac{ax}{b}| < 1 \Rightarrow |x| < \frac{b}{a}$

Procedure or Geogebra applets for plotting the graph of $\log(ax + b)$

Step 1: Open the geogebra classic 6 in your system.

Step 2: In the input bar, type $a = 1$, a slider for 'a' will come with defualt value from -5 to 5.

Step 3: Again, type $b = 1$ another slider for 'b' will came. The value of 'b' varies from -5 to 5.

Step 4: Next type the function $y = \log(b + ax)$.

Step 5: By changing the position of a and b in the slider. We can see the effect of a and b on the graph.

Observations

The graph of $y = \log(b + ax)$ is inverse of the graph of the function $y = e^{ax} + b$.

Conclusion

The graph of the function $y = \log(b + ax)$ is obtained as shown in figure 1.2

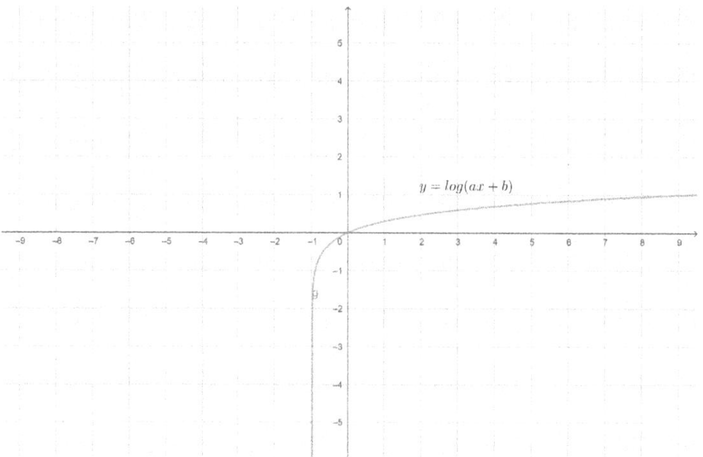

Figure 1.2: Graph of the function $y = \log(b + ax)$

1.3 Graph of function $1/(ax + b)$ and illustrate the effect of a and b on the graph

System requirement:- (i) Windows OS or android Phone

(ii) Geogebra software

Prerequisite:

(i) Geogebra interface: How to use geogebra

(ii) Knowledge of inverse function.

The function $y = \frac{1}{(ax+b)}$ can also be written as $y = (ax + b)^{-1}$ where $x \neq \frac{-b}{a}$

Procedure or Geogebra applets for plotting the graph of $1/(ax + b)$

Step 1: Open the geogebra classic 6 in your system.

Step 2: In the input bar, type $a = 1$ then slider for 'a' come. The value of 'a' varies from -5 to 5.

Step 3: Again, type $b = 1$ another slider for 'b' will came. The value of 'b' varies from -5 to 5.

Step 4: Next type the function $y = \frac{1}{(ax+b)}$.

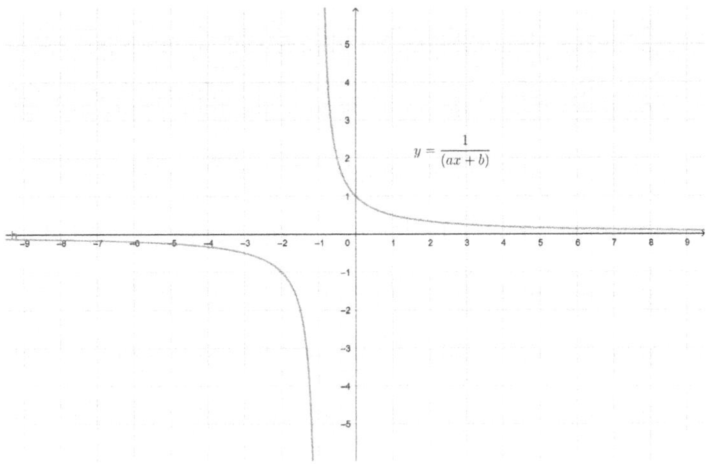

Figure 1.3: Graph of the function $y = \frac{1}{(ax+b)}$

Step 5: By changing the position of a and b in the slider. We can see the effect of a and b on the graph.

Observation

The graph of $y = \frac{1}{(ax+b)}$ is disconnected graph, one above positive $x-axes$ and other below positive $x-$axes.

Conclusion

The graph of the function $y = \frac{1}{(ax+b)}$ is obtained as shown in figure 1.3.

1.4 Graph of function $\sin(ax + b)$ and illustrate the effect of a and b on the graph

System requirement:- (i) Windows OS or android Phone

(ii) Geogebra software

Prerequisite: (i) Geogebra interface: How to use geogebra

(ii) Knowledge of sine function.

There are six basic trignometric functions used in trigonometry. They are- sine, cosine, secant, cosecant, tangent and cotangent.

Let $y = \sin(ax + b)$

differentiating wrt x using chain rule

$$\frac{dy}{dx} = \frac{d(\sin(ax+b))}{d(ax+b)} \cdot \frac{d(ax+b)}{dx} = a\cos(ax+b)$$

Procedure or Geogebra applets for plotting the graph of $\sin(ax+b)$

Step 1: Open the geogebra app in your system.

Step 2: In the input bar, type $a = 1$ then slider for 'a' will come. The default value of 'a' varies from -5 to 5.

Step 3: Again, type $b = 1$ another slider for 'b' will came. The default value of 'b' varies from -5 to 5.

Step 4: Change the x-axes to π or $\frac{\pi}{2}$. Right click on the axes in the graph then go to graphics and then go to xAxes tab and change label from x to θ and unit to π.

Step 5: Next type the function $y = \sin(ax + b)$.

Step 6: By changing the position of a and b in the slider. We can see the effect of a and b on the graph.

Observation

The graph of $y = \sin(ax + b)$ is wave forms. The curve is symmetrical about $x-$ axes

Conclusion

The graph of the function $y = \sin(ax + b)$ is obtained as shown in figure 1.4.

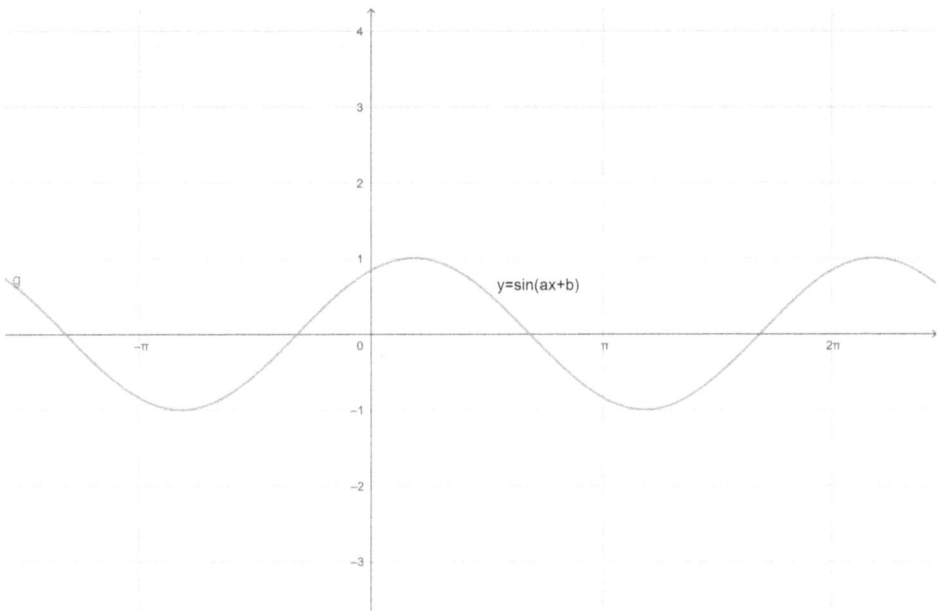

Figure 1.4: Graph of the function $y = \sin(ax + b)$

1.5 Graph of function $\cos(ax + b)$ and illustrate the effect of a and b on the graph

System requirement:- (i) Windows OS or android Phone

(ii) Geogebra software

Prerequisite: (i) Geogebra interface: How to use geogebra

(ii) Knowledge of cosine function. There are six basic trignometric functions used in trigonometry. They are- sine, cosine, secant, cosecant, tangent and cotangent.

Let $y = cos(ax + b)$

differentiating wrt x using chain rule

$\frac{dy}{dx} = \frac{d(\cos(ax+b))}{d(ax+b)} \cdot \frac{d(ax+b)}{dx} = -a\sin(ax + b)$

14

Procedure or Geogebra applets for plotting the graph of $\cos(ax + b)$

Step 1: Open the geogebra app in your system.

Step 2: In the input bar, type $a = 1$ then the slider for 'a' will come. The value of 'a' varies from -5 to 5.

Step 3: Again, type $b = 1$ another slider for 'b' will came. The value of 'b' varies from -5 to 5.

Step 4: Change the x-axes to π or $\frac{\pi}{2}$. Right click on the axes in the graph then go to graphics and then go to xAxes tab and change label from x to θ and unit to π.

Step 5: Next type the function $y = \cos(ax + b)$.

Step 5: By changing the position of a and b in the slider. We can see the effect of a and b on the graph.

Observations

The graph of $y = \cos(ax + b)$ is wave forms. The curve is symmetrical about $x-$ axes and range lies between ± 1

Conclusion

The graph of the function $y = \cos(ax + b)$ is obtained as shown in figure 1.5

1.6 Graph of the function $|ax + b|$ and illustrate the effect of a and b on the graph

System requirement:- (i) Windows OS or android phone

(ii) Geogebra software

Prerequisite: (i) Geogebra interface: How to use geogebra

(ii) Knowledge of modolus function.

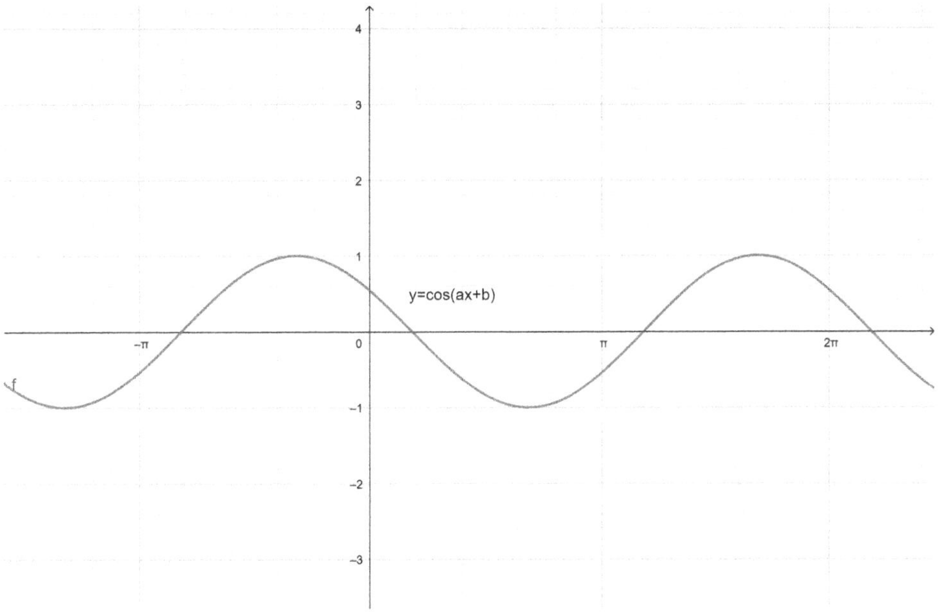

Figure 1.5: Graph of the function $y = \cos(ax + b)$

Modolus Function

$f(x) = |ax + b|$

$$f(x) = \begin{cases} ax + b, & \text{if } ax + b > 0; \\ 0, & \text{if } ax + b = 0 \\ -(ax + b), & \text{if } ax + b < 0 \end{cases}$$

$ax + b > 0 \Rightarrow x > \frac{-b}{a}$ where $ax + b \neq 0 \Rightarrow x \neq \frac{-b}{a}$

$ax + b = 0 \Rightarrow x = \frac{-b}{a}$

$-(ax + b) < 0 \Rightarrow x < \frac{-a}{b}$ where $ax + b \neq 0 \Rightarrow x \neq \frac{-b}{a}$

Procedure or Geogebra applets for plotting the modulus function

Step 1: Open the geogebra app in your system.

Step 2: In the input bar, type $a = 1$ then a slider for 'a' come. The value of 'a' varies from -5 to 5.

Step 3: Again, type $b = 1$ then another slider for 'b' will came. The value of 'b' varies from -5 to 5.

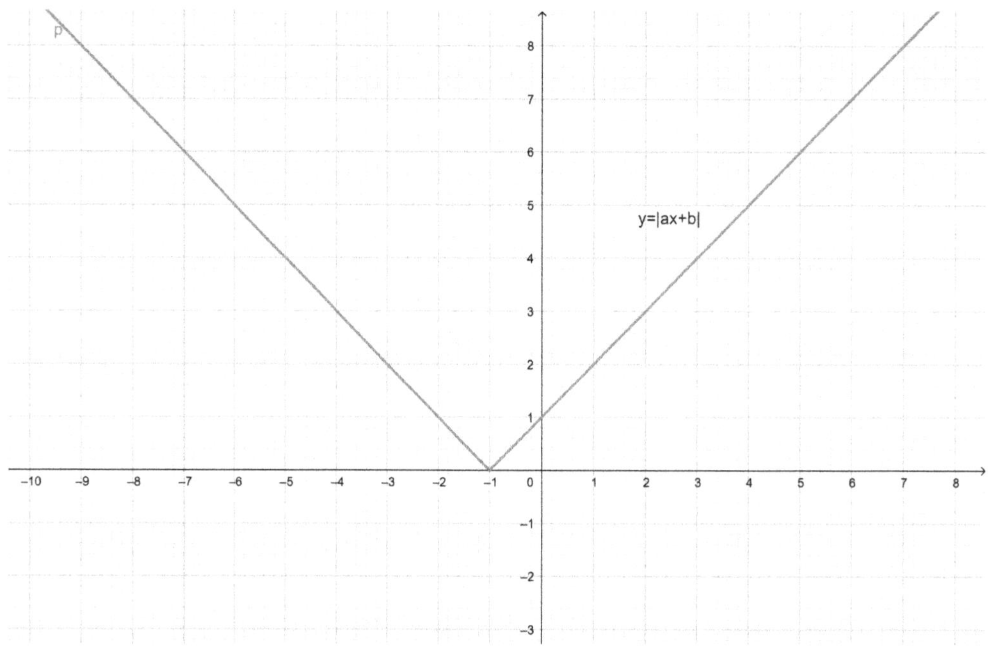

Figure 1.6: Graph of the function $y = |ax + b|$

Step 4: Next type the function $y = |ax + b|$.

Step 5: By changing the position of a and b in the slider. We can see the effect of a and b on the graph.

Observations

(i) The graph of $y = |ax + b|$ forms a $V-$shaped line.

(ii) When $a = 0$ the graph is a straight line through $y = b$ and is parallel to x-axes.

(iii) When $a = b = 0$ the graph is the $x-$axes.

Conclusion

The graph of the function $y = |ax + b|$ is obtained as shown in figure 1.6.

Chapter 2

Polynomials graph and there derivatives

In this chapter, we will discuss plotting of the graph of polynomials of degree 4 and 5 the derivative graph, the second derivative graph and comparing them

2.1 Tracing of Polynomial function

System requirement:- (i) Windows OS or Android Phone

(ii) Geogebra software

Prerequisite: (i) Geogebra interface: How to use geogebra

(ii) Knowledge of polynomial, derivatives of a function.

2.1.1 Polynomial

A polynomial is an expression in terms of variables and coefficient that involves the operation of addition, subtraction, multiplication; and the positive integer power of variables.

Derivative: The derivative of a function (of single variable) represent the slope of the tangent line to the graph of the function at the point. The tangent line is the best linear approximation of the function near that input value. For this reason the derivative is described as the ratio of the instantaneous rate of change in the dependent variable to that of the independent varible.

E.g. (i) 4th Degree Polynomial and its derivatives: $y = 3x^4 - 4x^3 + 5x^2 - 6x + 7$

$y' = 12x^3 - 12x^2 + 10x - 6$

$y'' = 36x^2 - 24x + 10$

$y''' = 72x - 24$

(ii) 5th Degree Polynomial:

$f(x) = (x - 1)(x + 1)(x + 1)(x + 2)(x + 2)$

2.1.2 Procedure or Geogebra applets for plotting of polynomial graph

Step 1: Open geogebra app in your system.

Step 2: In the input bar type the polynomial function i.e. $f(x) = \ldots$

Step 3: Type $n = 1$ a slider will come.

Step 4: Write a point A on the curve i.e. $A = (n, f(n))$

Step 5: Write tangent and within bracket the point A and polynomial function name i.e g=Tangent(A,f).

Step 6: Write Slope(g)

Step 7: Write $B = (n, a)$ where 'a' is the function name obtained in step 6.

Step 8: Right click on the point A and then click on show trace.

Step 9: Click on play button in n slider in step 3.

Step 10: Write $C = (n, f'(n))$

Step 11: Write $h = Tangent(C, f')$

Step 12: Write $b = Slope(h)$

Step 13: Write $D = (n, b)$

Step 14: Right click on the point D and then click on show trace and repeat step 9.

2.1.3   Observations

In 4th Degree polynomial

(i) A two line graph has formed

(ii) One line is $U-$shaped and the other is a straight line with two lines joining
at point A.

(iii) By writing again $f'(x)$ another line appears on point B.

(iv) A tangent is there with base 1 and length $a = 4$.

(v) By moving the n slider the tangent with point A and B changes.

In 5th Degree polynomial

(i) A three line graph has formed

(ii) One line in the graph is curve, one of the line is straight and the third is a
straight line with little curve.

(iii) A tangent is formed with base 1 and length $a = 4$.

(v) By moving the n in the slider the tangent will changes.

2.1.4   Conclusion

The graph of the polynomial and its derivatives are formed as shown in figure
2.1.

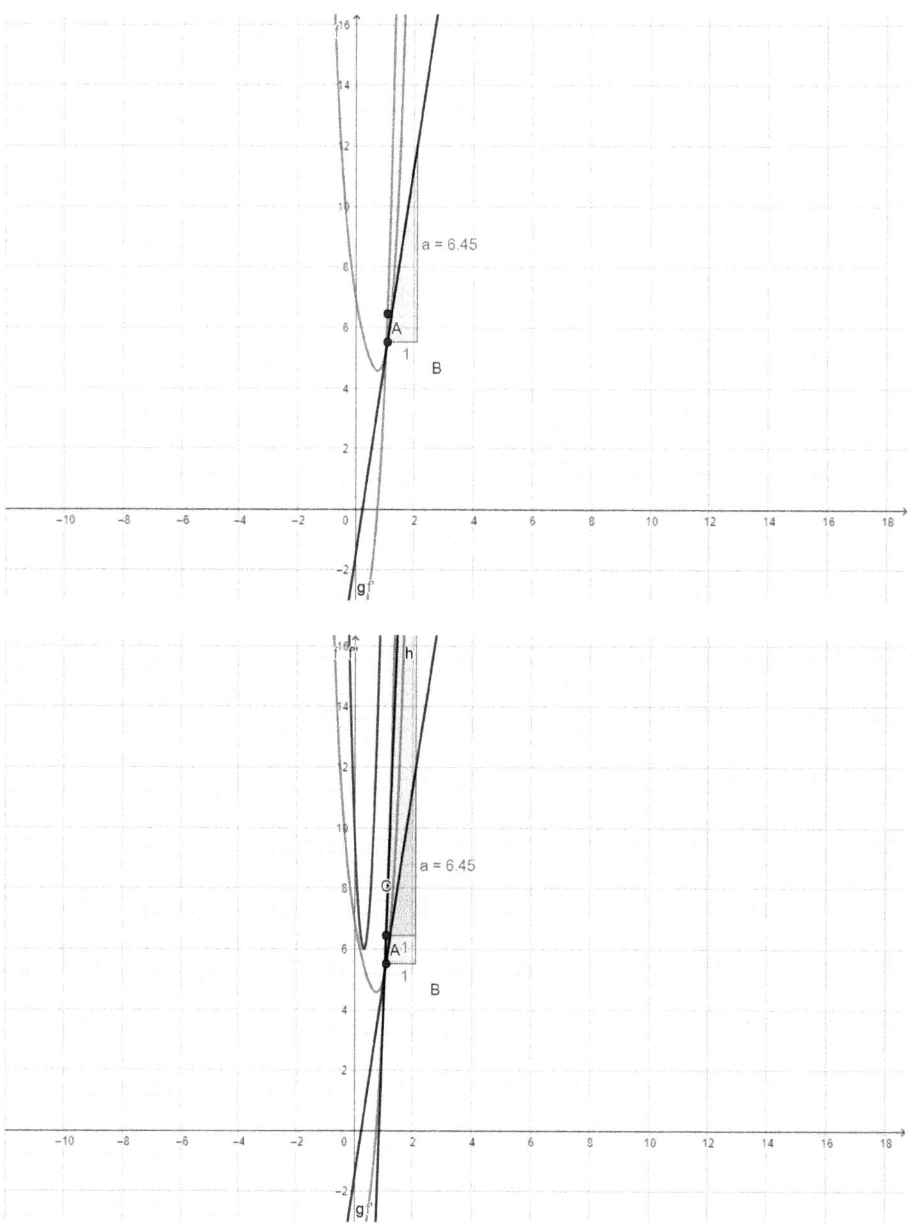

Figure 2.1: Derivative graph of 4th & 5th degree polynomial

Chapter 3

Sketching of parametric curves

In this chapter we will discuss how to Sketch parametric curve (Eg. Trochoid, cycloid, epicycloid, hypocycloid) using GeoGebra System requirement: (i) Windows OS or Android phone

(ii) Geogebra Classic 6

Pre requisite:

(i) Geogebra interface

(ii) Knowledge of parametric curves.

3.1 Sketching parametric equation of the circle

The parametric equation of circle with center as origin and radius a (i.e. $x^2 + y^2 = a^2$) is

$x = a\,cost,\ y = a\,sint$

3.1.1 Procedure or Geogebra applets

Step 1: Open geogebra app in your system.

Step 2: Type in the input bar, $t = 0$ then a slider will come, default value is -5 to 5 change the value of slider from 0 to 2π if you are unable to write π in your

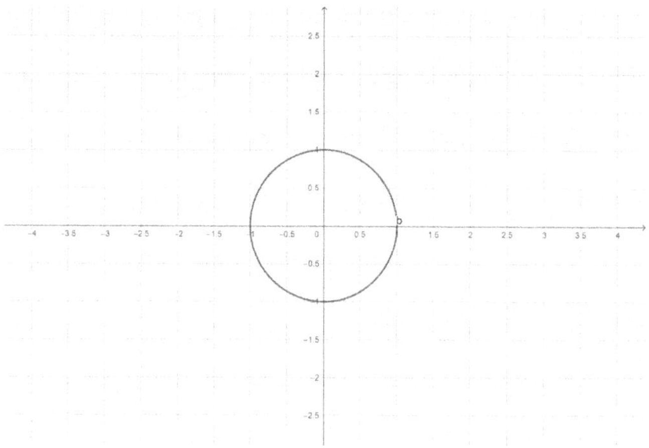

Figure 3.1: Curve of parametric equation of circle

system then take $\pi = 3.14$

Step 3: Again type $A = (a\cos t, a\sin t)$

Step 4: Click on the point A in the graph and click on show trace.

Step 5: Click on play button in the slider for t

3.1.2 Observations

(i) Size of circle increases with increase in value of a irrespective of its direction i.e. a is radius of the circle.

(ii) Origin is the center of the circle

3.1.3 Conclusion

The graph of the parametric equation of circle is obtained as shown in figure 3.1.

3.2 Sketching parametric equation of the parabola

General equation of parabola is $(y - k)^2 = 4a(x - h)$

changing to parametric equation

$$x = h + at^2, \ y = k + 2at$$

3.2.1 Procedure or Geogebra applets

Step 1: Open the geogebra app in your system.

Step 2: Type in the input bar, $a = 1$

Step 3: Type $h = 1$

Step 4: Type $k = 1$

Step 5: Type curve$(h + at^2, k + 2at, t, -4, 4)$

3.2.2 Observations:

(i) Vertex of the parabola shifted to (h, k)

(ii) If $h > 0$ parabola moves along positive x-axes

(iii) If $h < 0$ parabola moves along negative x-axes

(iv) If $k > 0$ parabola moves along upper half y-axes

(v) If $k < 0$ parabola moves along lower half y-axes

(vi) If $a < 0$ parabola open towards negative x-axes

(vii) If $a > 0$ parabola open towards pasitive x-axes

3.2.3 Conclusion

The graph of the parametric equation of parabola is obtained as shown in figure 3.2.

3.3 Sketching parametric equation of the ellipse

General equation of ellipse in cartesian coordinate is $\frac{(x-a)^2}{h^2} + \frac{(y-b)^2}{k^2} = 1$

Changing to parametric form,

Let $x = a + h\sin t, \ y = b + k\cos t$

Substituting these values of x, $\& \, y$ in cartesian equation of ellipse we get

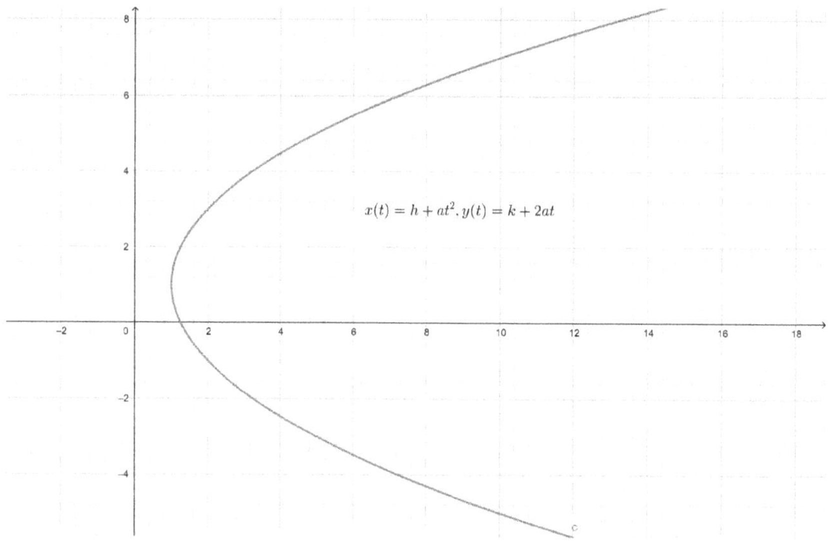

Figure 3.2: Curve of parametric equation of parabola

$$\frac{(a+h\sin t - a)^2}{h^2} + \frac{(b+k\cos t - b)^2}{k^2}$$
$$= \frac{(h\sin t)^2}{h^2} + \frac{(k\cos t)^2}{k^2}$$
$$= \sin^2 t + \cos^2 t$$
$$= 1$$

3.3.1   Procedure or Geogebra applets

Step 1: Open the geogebra app in your system.

Step 2: Type in the input bar, $t = 0$ change the value in the slider from 0 to 2π

Step 3: Again type $A = (a + h\sin t, b + k\cos t)$

Step 4: Click on the point A in the graph and click on show trace.

Step 5: Click on play button of the slider for t

Step 6: Instead of Step 4 & 5, you can write $curve(a + h\sin t, b + k\cos t, t, 0, 2\pi)$

3.3.2   Observations

(i) Vertex of the ellipse shifted to (h, k)

(ii) If $a < 0$ ellipse lies left of x-axes

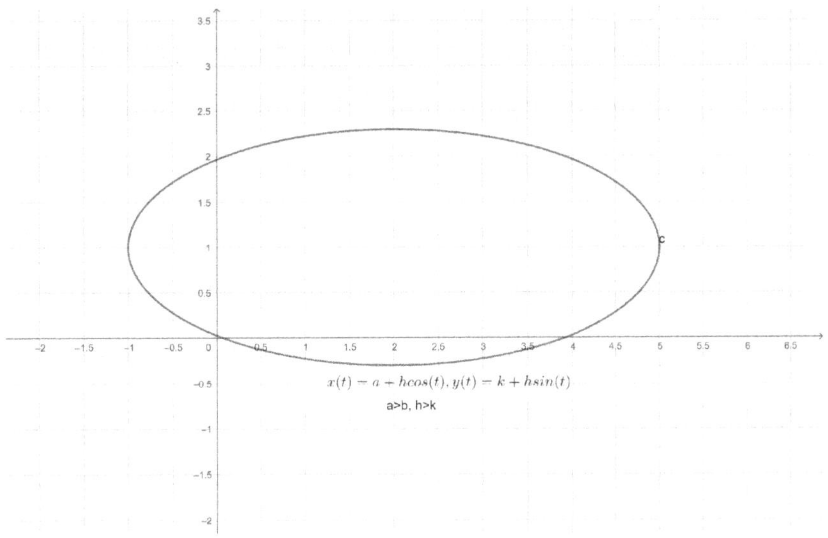

Figure 3.3: Curve of parametric equation of ellipse

(iii) If $a > 0$ ellipse lies right of x-axes

(iv) If $b > 0$ ellipse lies upper half of x-axes

(v) If $b < 0$ ellipse lies lower half of x-axes

(vi) If $h < k$ then the axes along y-axes

(vii) If $h > k$ then the axes along x-axes

3.3.3   Conclusion

The graph of the parametric equation of ellipse is obtained as shown in figure 3.3.

3.4   Sketching parametric equation of the hyperbola

General equation of hyperbola is $\frac{(x-h)^2}{a^2} - \frac{(y-k)^2}{b^2} = 1$

changing to parametric equation

$x = h + a\sec\theta$, $y = k + b\tan\theta$

3.4.1   Procedure or Geogebra applets

Step 1: Open the geogebra app in your system.

Step 2: Type in the input bar, $a = 1$

Step 3: Type $b = 1$

Step 4: Type $h = 1$

Step 5: Type $k = 1$

Step 4: Type curve$(h + a\sec\theta, k + b\tan\theta, \theta, 0, 2\pi)$

3.4.2   Observations

(i) Vetrex of the hyperbola shifted to (h, k)

(ii) If $a > b$ hyperbola is horizontal v shape

(iii) If $a < b$ hyperbola is flatter in shape

(iv) If h is negative hyperbola shifted to left side of x-axes

(v) If h is positive hyperbola shifted to right side of x-axes

(vi) If k is negative hyperbola shifted to lower half of y-axes

(v) If k is positive hyperbola shifted to upper half of y-axes

3.4.3   Conclusion

The graph of parametric equation of hyperbola is obtained as shown in figure
3.4.

3.5   Sketching parametric curve trochoid & cycloid:

The parametric equation of trochoid is

$$x = a\theta - b\sin\theta, \; y = a - b\cos\theta$$

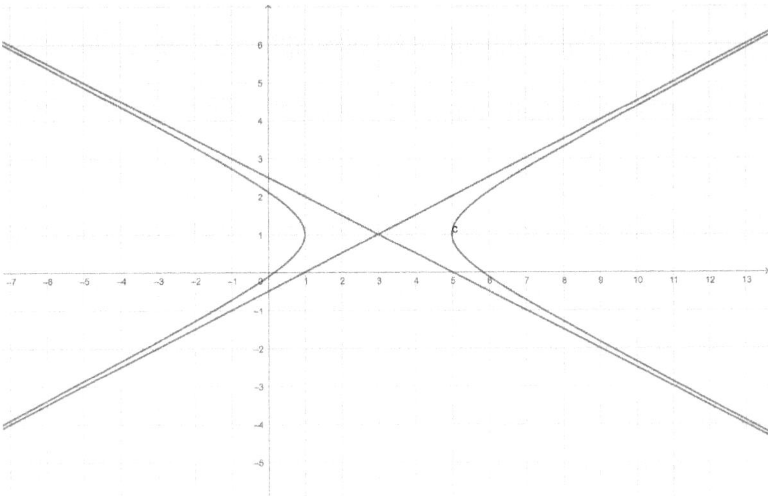

Figure 3.4: Curve of parametric equation of hyperbola

Procedure or geogebra applets

Step 1: Open geogebra app in your system

Step 2: Click on input bar and type $\theta = 1$ a slider will come. Change the value of slider from 0 to 5π.

As trochoid is nothing but path covered by bicycle wheel so to get the accurate picture we take more than two revolutions of the bicycle wheel i.e. value of θ more than 4π.

Step 3: Type $n = 0$ and change the value of slider from 0 to 5π or θ.

Step 4: Write $a = 1$ another slider will come, change the value of a to $0 \leq a \leq 5$ Here a started from 0 because path covered by bicycle wheel is never negative.

Step 5: Write $b = 1$ a new slider will come, change the value of b to $0 \leq b \leq 5$

Step 6: Type Curve$(a\theta - b\sin\theta, a - b\cos\theta, \theta, 0, n)$ and press enter

Step 7: go to n slider and θ slider and click on display button the graph will formed

3.5.1 Observations

(i) The curve formed is wave structure.

(ii) At $a = b$ the curve is cycloid

(iii) At $a > b$ the curve formed doesnot touch the x-axes

(iv) At $a < b$ the curve formed crosses the x-axes

3.5.2 Conclusion

The graph of the function is as shown in figure 3.5. There are three different resolutions for $a < b$, $a = b$, $\&a > b$

3.6 Sketching parametric curve epicycloid

The parametric equation of epicycloid

$$x(\theta) = (a + b)\cos\theta - b\cos(\frac{a + b}{b}\theta)$$

$$y(\theta) = (a + b)\sin\theta - b\sin(\frac{a + b}{b}\theta)$$

3.6.1 Procedure or geogebra applets

Step 1: Open geogebra app in your system

Step 2: Click on input bar and type $a = 4$, $2 \leq a \leq 8$

Step 3: Again type $b = 1$ and change the value of slider from 1 to 2

Step 4: Type $\theta = 4.19$, change the value of the slider $0 \leq \theta \leq 2\pi$

Step 5: Write Curve$(a\cos\theta, a\sin\theta, \theta, 0, 2\pi)$

Step 6: Write Curve$((a + b)\cos(\theta), (a + b)\sin\theta, \theta, 0, 2\pi)$

Remove select in input bar so that this circle should not appear in the graph

Step 7: Write Curve$((a+b)\cos\theta - b\cos(\frac{a+b}{b}\theta), (a+b)\sin\theta - b\sin(\frac{a+b}{b}\theta), \theta, 0, 2\pi)$

Step 8: write $\theta_1 = 1$

Step 9: $Q = c(\theta_1)$

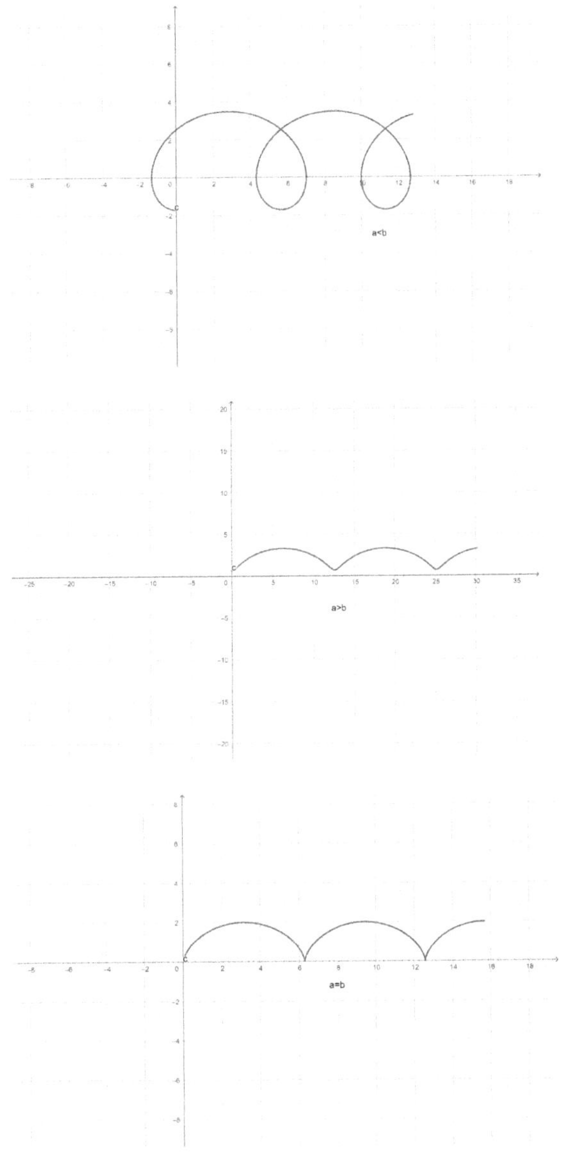

Figure 3.5: Trochoid when $a < b$, $a > b$, $\& a = b$

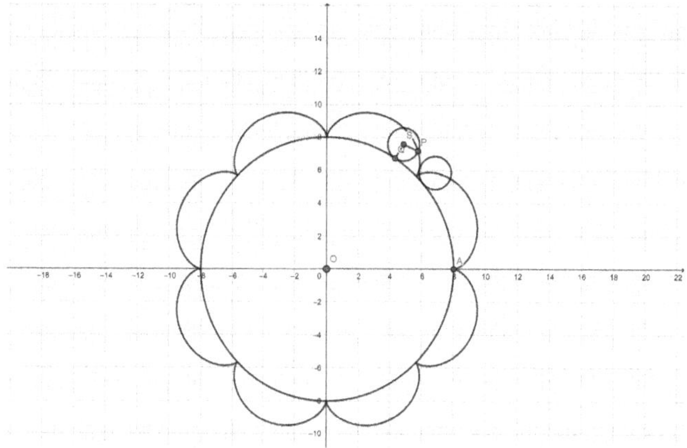

Figure 3.6: Graph of epicycloid

Step 10: $S = d(\theta_1)$

Step 11: $P = e(\theta_1)$

Step 12: $A = (a, 0)$

Step 13: f=Circle (S, P)

Step 14: g=Segment (Q, S)

Step 15: h=Segment (P, S)

Step 16: Rotate(f, θ)

3.6.2 Observations

(i) At $\frac{a}{b} = 1$ The curve formed by small circles on the bigger circle depends on the value of a and b. This is the reason for choosing a and b in step 2 and 3.

(ii) If $\frac{a}{b} > 1$ the number curve outside the circle increase as b decreases and number of curve form outside the circle is equal to the integer value of the ratio $\frac{a}{b}$

(iii) If $\frac{a}{b} > 1$, the number curve outside the circle decreases as b increases and number of curve form outside the circle is equal to the integer value of the ratio $\frac{a}{b}$

3.6.3 Conclusion

The curve obtain is epicycloid as shown in figure 3.6.

3.7   Sketching parametric curve hypocycloid

The parametric equation of hypocycloid

$$x(\theta) = (R - r)\cos\theta + r\cos(\frac{R - r}{r}\theta)$$

$$y(\theta) = (R - r)\sin\theta - r\sin(\frac{R - r}{r}\theta)$$

3.7.1   Procedure or geogebra applets

Step 1: Open geogebra app in your system

Step 2: In the input bar, type $R = 4$ Slide with default value -5 to 5 came, change the value from 2 to 8

Step 3: Type $r = 1$ change the default value of the slider from 1 to 2

Step 4: Type $Curve(R\cos\theta, R\sin\theta, \theta, 0, 2\pi)$

Step 5: Type $Curve((R - r)\cos\theta, (R - r)\sin\theta, \theta, 0, 2\pi)$

Step 6: Type $Curve((R-r)\cos\theta + r\cos(\frac{R-r}{r}\theta), (R-r)\sin\theta - r\sin(\frac{R-r}{r}\theta), \theta, 0, 2\pi)$

3.7.2   Observations

(i) Value of the ratio $\frac{R}{r} > 2$. This is the reason for choosing value of R and r in step 2 and step 3

(ii) At $\frac{R}{r} = 2$ the inner curve is a straight line

(iii) If $\frac{R}{r} > 2$ the number of inner curve formed is depends on the value of r, larger the value of r less will be number of inner curve formed it is equal to integer value of the ratio $\frac{R}{r}$ and smaller the value of r more will be the number of inner curve formed and it is again equal to the integer value of the ratio $\frac{R}{r}$.

3.7.3   Conclusion

The graph obtained is hypocycloid as shown in figure 3.7.

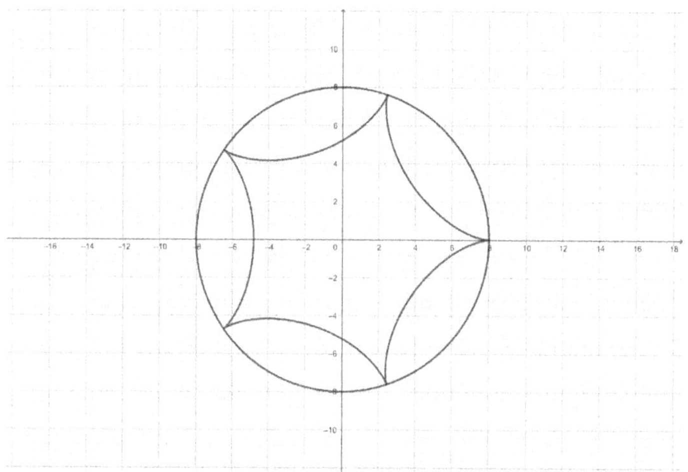

Figure 3.7: Graph of hypocycloid

Chapter 4

Surface of revolution

In this chapter we will discuss how to obtain surface of revolution of curves and to obtain there surface integral. If a plane curve is revolved about a fixed line lying in its own plane, then the surface generated by the parameter of the curve is called a surface of revolution.

Surface of revolution about $x - axes$

The surface of solid of revolution obtained by revolution of the curve $y = f(x)$ along the $x - axes$ between points $x = a$ to $x = b$ is

$$\int_{x=a}^{x=b} 2\pi y ds$$

$$= \int_a^b 2\pi y \frac{ds}{dx} dx$$
$$= \int_a^b 2\pi y \sqrt{1 + (\frac{dy}{dx})^2}.dx$$

The surface of solid of revolution obtained by revolution of the curve $x = g(y)$ along the $y - axes$ between points $y = a$ to $y = b$ is

$$\int_{y=c}^{y=d} 2\pi x ds$$

$$= \int_c^d 2\pi x \frac{ds}{dy} dy$$
$$= \int_c^d 2\pi x \sqrt{1 + (\frac{dx}{dy})^2}.dy$$

In parametric form

If the equation of the curve is

$x = f(x),\ y = \phi(t),\ a \leq t \leq b$

Then surface of the solid of revolution formed is $= 2\pi \int_{t_1}^{t_2} y \frac{ds}{dt}.dt$

where $\frac{ds}{dt} = \sqrt{(\frac{dx}{dt})^2 + (\frac{dy}{dt})^2}.dt$

In Polar form:

If the equation of the curve in the polar form $r = f(\theta)$. Then the surface of the solid form by revolution between $\theta = \alpha$ to $\theta = \beta$ is

$\int_{\alpha}^{\beta} 2\pi(r\sin(\theta)) \frac{ds}{d\theta}.d\theta$

where $\frac{ds}{d\theta} = \sqrt{r^2 + (\frac{dr}{d\theta})^2}$

4.1 Surface of revolution of parabola

System requirement: (i) Windows OS and android phone

(ii) Geogebra Classic 6

Pre requisite:

(i) Geogebra interface

(ii) Knowledge of parabola.

Surface of revolution of parabola about $x - axes$ between the latus rectum $y = -a$ to $y = a$ is

We know the equation of parabola is $y^2 = 4ax \Rightarrow y = \sqrt{4ax}$

$\therefore$ Surface area$= \int_{x=-a}^{x=a} 2\pi y ds == \int_a^b 2\pi y \sqrt{1 + (\frac{dy}{dx})^2}.dx = \int_a^b 2\pi 2\sqrt{ax} \sqrt{1 + (\frac{1}{2}2\sqrt{\frac{a}{x}})^2}.dx = \int_a^b 2\pi 2\sqrt{ax} \sqrt{1 + \frac{a}{x}}.dx = 4\pi\sqrt{a} \int_{-a}^a \sqrt{x+a}dx$

4.1.1 Procedure or Geogebra applets

Step 1: Open 3D graphic in geogebra app in your system.

Step 2: Type $a = 1$ a slider will come with default value -5 to 5

Step 3: Type $n = 1$ change the value in corresponding slider from 0 to 20

Step 4: In the input bar, type the function $f(x) = \sqrt{4ax}$

Step 5: Again in the input bar type Surface$(f, n, x - Axes)$

Step 6: For calculating area of surface, open CAS in geogebra app

Step 7: write the command integral(function, Variable, start value, end value) to obtain value of surface

Here, function is the integrand$=4\pi\sqrt{a}\sqrt{x+a}$, variable=x, start value=$-a$, end

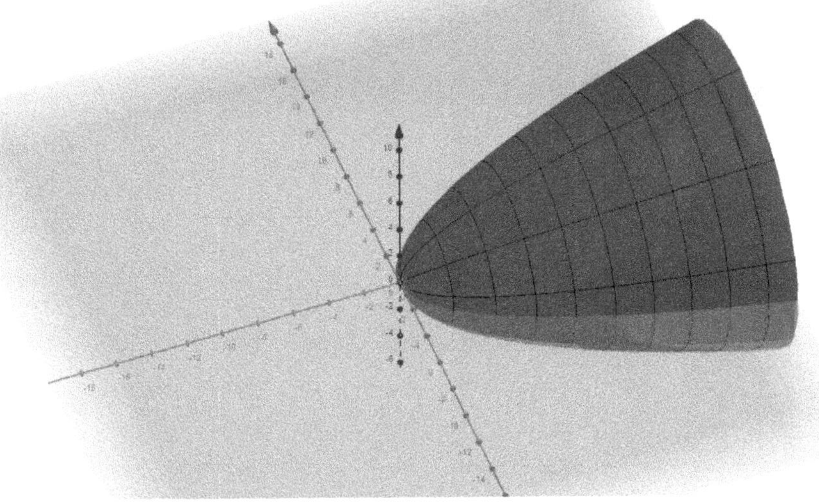

Figure 4.1: Surface of revolution of parabola

value=a

$\therefore$ Surface area $= \frac{16}{3}\pi a^2 \sqrt{2}$

4.1.2 Observations

(i) The Surface formed by the revolution of parabola about x-axes is appears as hollow bowl

(ii) The surface open toward x-axes

4.1.3 Conclusion

The surface of revolution of parabola is shown in figure 4.1 and surface area is calculated using CAS in geogebra which reduced time as well as complexity of computation.

4.2   Surface of revolution of ellipse

System requirement: (i) Windows OS and android phone

(ii) Geogebra Classic 6

Pre requisite:

(i) Geogebra interface

(ii) Knowledge of ellipse

Equation of ellipse is

$\frac{x^2}{a^2} + \frac{y^2}{b^2} = 1 \Rightarrow y = b\sqrt{(1 - \frac{x^2}{a^2})}$

Ellipse is symmetrical about both the axes.

Therefore, surface of revolution of ellipse about $x-axes$ is $= 2\int_0^a 2\pi y\sqrt{1 + (\frac{dy}{dx})^2}.dx = 4\pi\frac{b}{a^2}\int_0^a \sqrt{a^4 + (b^2 - a^2)x^2}dx$

4.2.1   Procedure or Geogebra applets

Step 1: Open 3D graphics in geogebra app in your system.

Step 2: write $a = 1$ a slider will come with default value -5 to 5

Step 3: write $b = 1$ a slider will come with default value -5 to 5

Step 4: write $n = 1$ the value in the slider from 0 to 20

Step 5: In the input bar, type the function $f(x) = b\sqrt{(1 - \frac{x^2}{a^2})}$

Step 6: Again in the input bar type surface(f,n, xAxes)

Step 7: For calculating area of surface, open CAS in geogebra app

Step 8: write the command Integral(function, Variable,start value, end value) to obtain value of surface

Here function is the integrand $4\pi\frac{b}{a^2}\sqrt{a^4 + (b^2 - a^2)x^2}$, variable is x, start value is 0, end value is a

surface area is $2\pi\frac{b}{a^2\sqrt{b^2-a^2}}\{-a^4\log{(\sqrt{a^2b^2} - a\sqrt{b^2 - a^2})} + a\sqrt{a^2b^2(b^2 - a^2)} + a^4\log a^2\}$

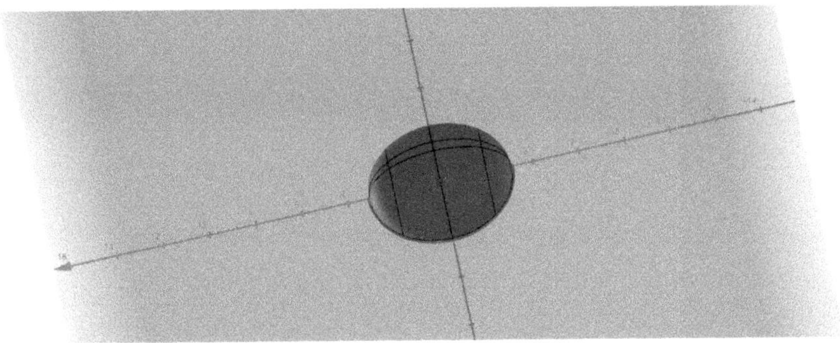

Figure 4.2: Surface of revolution of ellipse

4.2.2 Observations

(i) The surface formed by the revolution of ellipse about the x-axes is appears as hollow oval soccer ball.

(ii) The surface increases in size as change the value of a, b, increases.

(iii) The surface is along x-axes if $a > b$ and along y-axes if $a < b$.

4.2.3 Conclusion

The surface of revolution of ellipse about x-axes is shown in figure 4.2 and surface area is calculated by using CAS.

4.3 Surface of revolution of hyperbola

System requirement: Windows OS and android phone

(ii) Geogebra Classic 6

Pre requisite:

(i) Geogebra interface

(ii) Knowledge of hyperbola

Surface of revolution of hyperbola about $x - axes$ whose standard equation is

$$\frac{x^2}{a^2} - \frac{y^2}{b^2} = 1 \Rightarrow y = b\sqrt{\left(\frac{x^2}{a^2}\right) - 1} = \frac{b}{a}\sqrt{x^2 - a^2}$$

$$\text{Surface area} == \int_a^b 2\pi y \sqrt{1 + \left(\frac{dy}{dx}\right)^2}.dx = 2\int_0^a 2\pi \frac{b}{a^2} \sqrt{(a^2 + b^2)x^2 - a^4}\,dx$$

4.3.1 Procedure or Geogebra applets:

Step 1: Open 3D graphics in geogebra app in your system.

Step 2: write $a = 1$, slider will come, its value varies from -5 to 5

Step 3: write $b = 1$, slide will come, its value varies from -5 to 5

Step 4: Write $n = 1$ change the value in the slider from 0 to 10

Step 5: In the input bar type the function $f(x) = b\sqrt{\left(\frac{x^2}{a^2}\right) - 1}$

Step 6: Again type Surface(f, n, xAxes)

Step 7: For calculating area of surface, open CAS in geogebra app

Step 8: write the command Integral(function, Variable,start value, end value) to obtain value of surface

Here function is the integrand $4\pi \frac{b}{a^2} \sqrt{(a^2 + b^2)x^2 - a^4}$, variable is x, start value is 0 end value is a

$$\text{surface area} = 2\pi \frac{b}{a^2\sqrt{a^2+b^2}} \left\{ a^4 \log(\sqrt{a^2 b^2} - a\sqrt{a^2 + b^2}) + a\sqrt{a^2 b^2 (a^2 + b^2)} - \frac{1}{2}a^4 \log a^4 \right\}$$

4.3.2 Observations

(i) The surface of revolution of hyperbola appears as two hollow bowl place at end to end and face of bowl facing opposite to each other.

(ii) The surface lies along x-axes if $a > b$ and along y-axes if $a < b$.

(iii) The surface increases in size as change the value of a, b, increases.

4.3.3 Conclusion

The surface of revolution of hyperbola about x-axes is shown in figure 4.3 and surface area is calculated by using CAS.

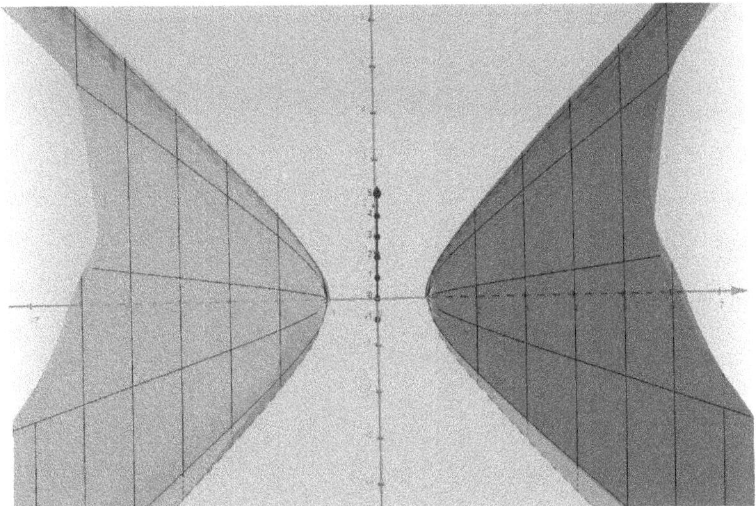

Figure 4.3: Surface of revolution of hyperbola

4.4 Surface of revolution of circle using polar equation

System requirement:- (i) Windows OS or Android Phone

(ii) Geogebra software.

Prerequisite:

(i) Geogebra interface: How to use geogebra

(ii) Knowledge of integrals and polar equation of circle.

Equation of circle in polar form is $r = 2a\cos\theta$.

Circle is symmetrical about initial line. For the upper half of the curve θ varies from 0 to $\frac{\pi}{2}$. Therefore surface of revolution of the circle about the initial line is $= \int_0^{\frac{\pi}{2}} 2\pi y \frac{ds}{d\theta}\theta$ where $\frac{ds}{d\theta}$

$= \sqrt{r^2 + (\frac{dr}{d\theta})^2} = 8\pi a^2 \int_0^{\frac{\pi}{2}} \cos\theta\sin\theta d\theta$

4.4.1 Procedure or Geogebra applets

Step 1: Open 3D graphics in geogebra app in your system.

Step 2: write $a = 1$

Step 3: write curve $r = 2a\cos\theta$ in the input bar. System will give the curve some name say b

Step 4: Spin=1, $0 \leq Spin \leq 2\pi$

Step 5: Surface(b, Spin)

Step 6: For surface area, click on CAS in geogebra app

Step 7: Write Integral(function, variable, start value, end value)

function=$8\pi a^2 \cos\theta \sin\theta d\theta$, variable=$\theta$,

start value=0, end value=$\frac{\pi}{2}$

$\therefore$ surface area $= 4\pi a^2$

4.4.2   Observations

(i) The surface obtain by revolution of the circle about initial line is sphere.

(ii) The sphere increase in radius with increase in value of a along positive axes

(iii) The sphere increase in radius with decrease in value of a along negative axes

4.4.3   Conclusion

The surface generated by revolution of the give curve is a sphere touching the origin as shown in figure 4.4.3 and surface area of the sphere of revolution is obtained by using CAS which reduced the time of computation.

4.5   Surface of revolution of cardioid using polar equation

System requirement:- (i) windows OS or android Phone

(ii) Geogebra classic 6

Prerequisite:

(i) Geogebra interface: How to use geogebra

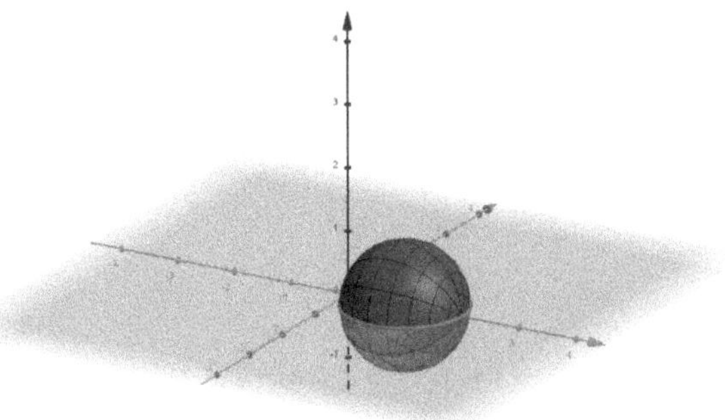

Figure 4.4: Surface of revolution of cirle

(ii) Knowledge of integrals and polar curves.

Polar equation of cardioid is $r = a(1 + cos(\theta))$
A cardioid is symmetrical about the initial line and for the upper half of the curve θ varies from 0 to π Surface area of cardiod about the initial line is
$= \int_0^\pi 2\pi r \sin\theta \frac{ds}{d\theta} d\theta$ where $\frac{ds}{d\theta} = \sqrt{r^2 + (\frac{dr}{d\theta})^2}$
$= 16\pi a^2 \int_0^\pi \cos^4\theta \sin\theta d\theta$

4.5.1 Procedure or Geogebra applets

Step 1: Open 3D graphics in geogebra app in your system.

Step 3: Write $a = 1$

Step 4: Write curve $r = a(1+\cos\theta)$ in the input bar. System will give the curve some name say b

Step 5: Spin=1, $0 \le Spin \le 2\pi$

Step 6: Surface(b, Spin)

Step 7: For surface area, click on CAS in geogebra

Step 8: Write Integral(function, variable, start value, end value)

function$= 16\pi a^2 \cos^4\theta \sin\theta$, variable $= \theta$,

start value $= 0$, end value $= \pi$

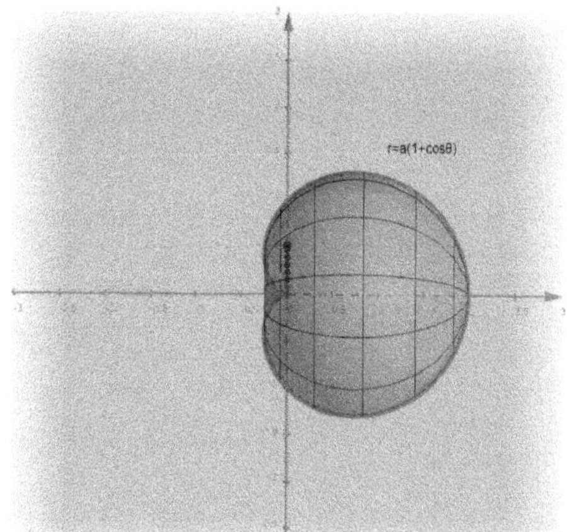

Figure 4.5: Surface of revolution of cardioid

$\therefore$ Surface area$=\frac{32}{5}\pi a^2$

4.5.2   Observations

(i) The surface obtained by revolution cardioid is a hollow heart like shape structure

(ii) For $a > 0$ cardioid increases with increase value of a along positive orientation

(iii) For $a > 0$ cardioid increases with decrease in value of a along negative orientation

4.5.3   Conclusion

Surface of revolution of cardioid is as shown in figure 4.5 and surface area is obtained by CAS which make the calculation much more easier.

4.6   Surface of revolution of parametric curves

System requirement:- (i) Windows OS or Android Phone

(ii) Geogebra software

Prerequisite:

(i) Geogebra interface: How to use geogebra

(ii) Knowledge about indefinite and definite integrals, and parametric curves.

The parametric curve considered here is astroid. We know the parametric equation of astroid is

$x = a\cos^3 t,\ y = a\sin^3 t,\ 0 \le t \le 2\pi$

Astroid is symmetrical about both the axes and in the first quadrant t varies from 0 to $\frac{\pi}{2}$. Surface area of astroid about $x-$axes is

$= 2\int_0^{\frac{\pi}{2}} 2\pi y \frac{ds}{dx}$ where $\frac{ds}{dx} = \sqrt{(\frac{dx}{dt})^2 + (\frac{dy}{dt})^2}$

$= 12\pi a^2 \int_{-\frac{\pi}{2}}^{\frac{\pi}{2}} \sin^4 t \cos t\, dt$

4.6.1   Procedure or Geogebra applets

Step 1: Open 3D graphics in geogebra app in your system.

Step 2: write Curve $(a\cos^3 t, a\sin^3 t, t, 0, 2\pi)$

Step 3: Spin=1, $0 \le Spin \le 2\pi$

Step 4: Surface(f, Spin, xAxes)

Step 5: For calculation of surface area, open CAS in geogebra app

Step 6: Write the command Integral(function, variable, start value, end value)

In this case function=$12\pi a^2 \sin^4 t \cos t$, variable=$t$, start value=0, end value $=\frac{\pi}{2}$

$\therefore$ Surface area $=\frac{12}{5}\pi a^2$

4.6.2   Observations

(i) The size of surface of revolution does not depend on sign of a.

(ii) The astroid is symmetrical about both the axes.

(iii) Surface area is $\frac{32}{5}\pi a^2$

4.6.3   Conclusion

Surface obtained by revolution of astroid is as shown in figure 4.6 and surface area is calculated by CAS.

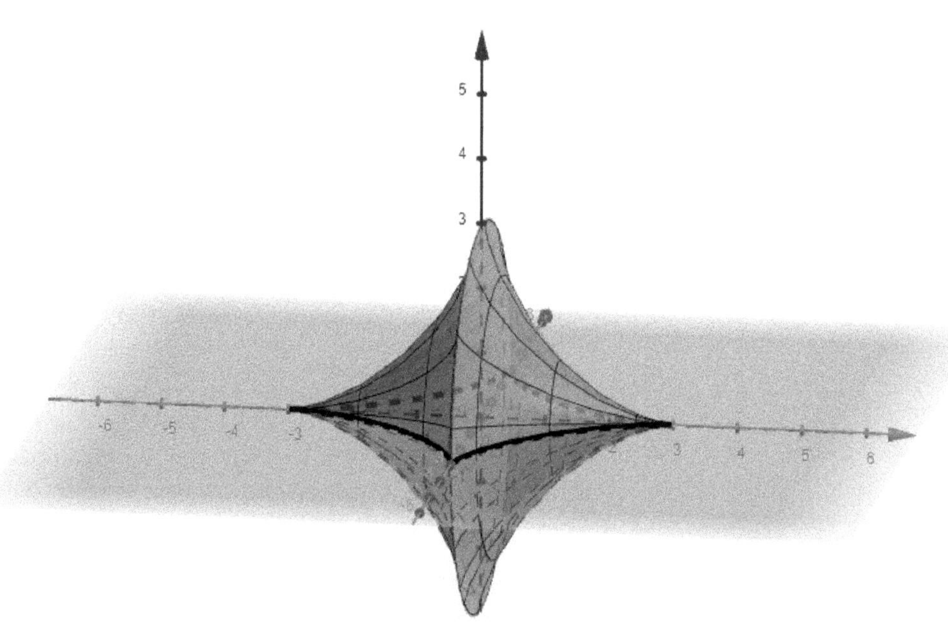

Figure 4.6: Surface of revolution of astroid

Chapter 5

Tracing of conics in cartesian & polar coordinates

In this chapter we will discuss tracing of conics in cartesian and polar coordinates

5.1 Tracing of circle in cartesian coordinate

System requirement:

(i) Windows OS or android phone

(ii) Geogebra Classic 6

Pre requisite:

(i) Geogebra interface

(ii) Knowledge of circle.

Equation of a circle with centre at (h, k) & radius r

$(x - h)^2 + (y - k)^2 = r^2$

5.1.1 Procedure or geogebra applets

Step 1: Open geogebra classic 6 in your system.

Step 2: In the input bar we type $h = 1$ then the slider h will come and the value of the slider varies from -5 to 5.

Step 3: Again, type $k = 1$ then another slider for k will come with value varies

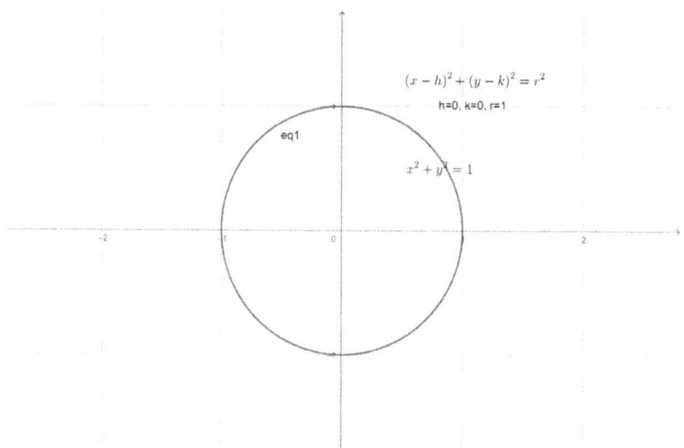

Figure 5.1: Circle in cartesian coordinate

from -5 to 5.

Step 4: Again, type $r = 1$ then the slider r will come, the default value of r varies from -5 to 5.

Step 5: Next, type the function $(x - h)^2 + (y - k)^2 = r^2$

Step 6: By changing the position of $a, b \,\&\, r$ in the slider we can see the change in the graph.

5.1.2   Observations

(i) The graph of the equation $(x - h)^2 + (y - k)^2 = r^2$ from a circle.

(ii) When the value of r decreases the circle in the graph decrease and when $r = 0$ the circle is a point in the origin.

(iii) The size of the circle increases as the value of r increases.

5.1.3   Conclusion

The graph of circle obtained is shown in figure 5.1

5.2   Tracing of parabola in cartesian coordinate

System requirement: Windows OS and Geogebra Classic 6

Pre requisite:

(i) Geogebra interface

(ii) Knowledge of parabola.

A parabola is the set of point in a plane that are equidistant from a fixed line and a fixed point (not on the line) in the plane.

The fixed line is called the directive of the parabola & the fixed point F is called the focus. A line through the focus and perpendicular to the directrix is called the axes of the parabola. The point of intersection of parabola with the axes is called the vertex of the parabola.

Let $P(x, y)$ be any point on parabola, focus $(a, 0)$ and $(-a, y)$ be coordinate of any point B such that $PF = PB$

By distance formmula

$$PF = \sqrt{(x-a)^2 + y^2}$$
$$PB = \sqrt{(x+a)^2}$$
$$\therefore PF = PB$$
$$\sqrt{(x-a)^2 + y^2} = \sqrt{(x+a)^2}$$
$$\Rightarrow (x-a)^2 + y^2 = (x+a)^2$$
$$\Rightarrow x^2 - 2ax + a^2 + y^2 = x^2 + 2ax + a^2$$

$y^2 = 4ax$ is the equation of parabola.

5.2.1   Procedure or geogebra applets

Step 1: Open the geogebra classic 6 in your system.

Step 2: In the input bar, type $P = 1$ then a slider with default value -5 to 5 will come.

Step 3: Then type $Focus = (P, 0)$ in the input bar.

Step 4: Type $x = -P$

Step 5: Next we go the tool bar and click on parabola.

Step 6: Then we click on focus and the line $x = -P$ (directrix). Graph of parabola will come.

Step 7: Type $Vertex(conic)$. the term 'conic' in the bracket is replaced by function name of the conic obtained in step 5.

Step 8: Click on point in tool bar and write a point on the parabola.

Step 9: Click on segment and draw the segment from focus to the point on parabola.

Step 10: Go to tool bar and click on perpendicular and draw a perpendicular from the point on the parabola to the directrix.

Step 11: Again go to tool bar, click on intersect then click on intersection point of perpendicular from point on the parabola to the directrix.

Step 12: Click on segment and join the line segement from intersection point to the point on the parabola.

Step 13: Click on line outside the line joining the line segement from intersection point to the point on the parabola and right click over it and click on show object.

5.2.2   Observations

(i) The graph of $y^2 = 4ax$ forms a parabola on the positive $x-$axes.

(ii) If a is less than 0 then the graph face open towards the left side of the axes.

(iii) If a is greater than 0 then the graph face open towards the right side of the axes.

(iv) When $a = 0$ the arc turns into a straight line on the $x-$axes of the graph.

5.2.3   Conclusion

we trace the graph of parabola in cartesian coordinate as shown in figure 5.2.

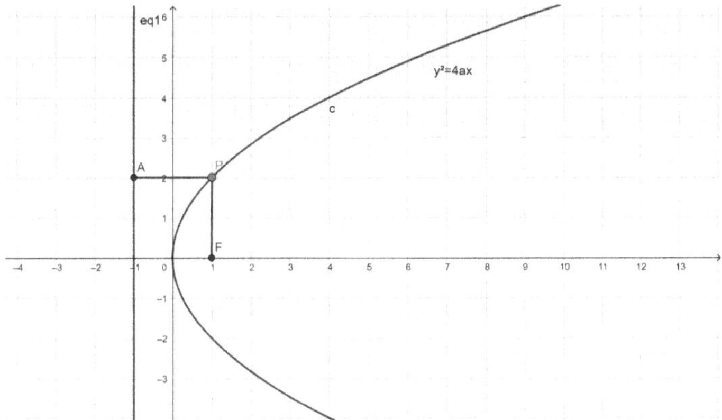

Figure 5.2: Parabola in cartesian coordinate

5.3 Tracing of ellipse in cartesian coordinate

System requirement:(i) Windows OS and android phone

(ii) Geogebra Classic 6

Pre requisite:

(i) Geogebra interface

(ii) Knowledge of a circle.

Ellipse: An ellipse is the set of all points in a plane, the sum of whose distance from two fixed points in the plane is a constant. The two fixed points are called the foci of the ellipse.

Equation of ellipse with semi major axis along $x-$aaxes and semi minor axis along $y-$axes is

$\frac{x^2}{a^2} + \frac{y^2}{b^2} = 1, a > b$

In particular to draw the graph we take $a = 4, b = 3$ so that equation of ellipse becomes $\frac{x^2}{16} + \frac{y^2}{9} = 1$

5.3.1 Procedure or geogebra applets

Step 1: Open geogebra app in your system.

Step 2: In the input bar, type the function $\frac{x^2}{a^2} + \frac{y^2}{b^2} = 1$

Step 3: In the input bar, type $P = $ Point(conic) where the conic is function name obtained in step 2.

Step 3: In the input bar, type $Q = $ Point(conic) where the conic is function name obtained in step 2.

Sometime points P and Q are overlap then go to move button in tool bar and click on move then click on the point in the graph which you want to move.

Step 4: Type $A1 = (-a, 0)$ and press enter

Step 5: Type $A2 = (a, 0)$

Step 6: Type $B1 = (0, -b)$

Step 7: Type $B2 = (0, b)$

Step 8: Type $F1 = (-\sqrt{(a^2 - b^2)}, 0)$

Step 9: Type $F2 = (\sqrt{(a^2 - b^2)}, 0)$

Step 10: Click on segment and join the point $PF1$ and $PF2$; then right click over the line $PF1$ and $PF2$, goto setting click on it and change show label to value and closed it

Step 11: Click on segment and join the point $QF1$ and $QF2$ and repeat step 10 for $QF1$ and $QF2$

Step 12: Click on play button in step 3&4 (horizontal triangle mark) to verify
$$\sqrt{(PF1)^2 + (PF2)^2} = \sqrt{(QF1)^2 + (QF2)^2}$$

5.3.2   Observations

(i) When $a = 4$ & $b = 3$ the curve is an ellipse.

(ii) When $a = b = 1$ the ellipse turns into a unit circle.

(iii) When $a = b = 0$ the figure in the graph disappears.

5.3.3   Conclusion

We trace the graph of ellipse in cartesian coordinate as shown in figure 5.3.

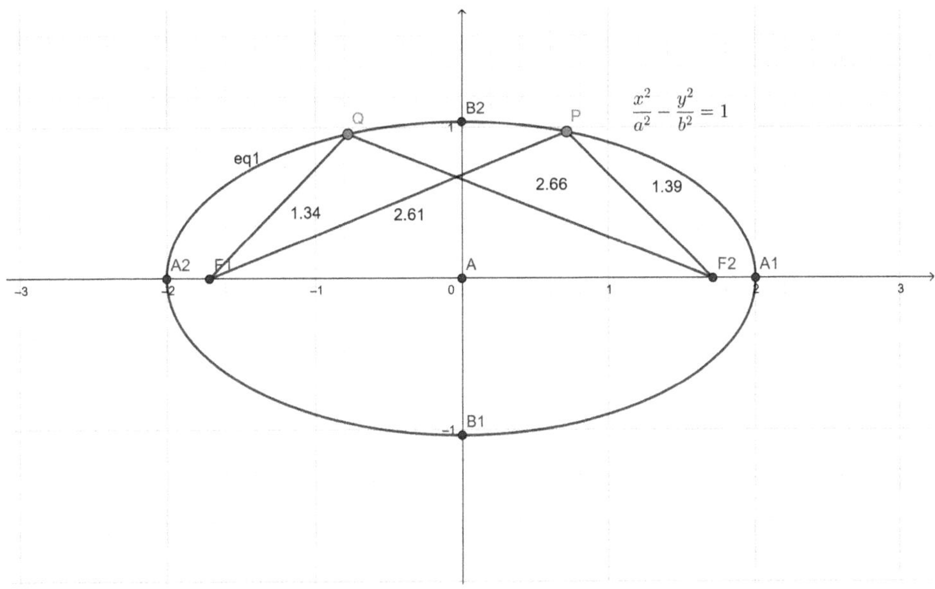

Figure 5.3: Ellipse in cartesian coordinates

5.4 Tracing of hyperbola in cartesian coordinate

System requirement: (i) Windows OS or android phone

(ii) Geogebra Classic 6

Pre requisite:

(i) Geogebra interface

(ii) Knowledge of hyperbola.

A hyperbola is the set of all points in a plane the difference of whose distance from two points in the plane is a constant. The two fixed points are called the foci of hyperbola.

Equation of hyperbola with conjugate axis along $x-$axis and minor axis along $y-$axis is $\frac{x^2}{a^2} - \frac{y^2}{b^2} = 1$, $a > b$

5.4.1 Procedure or geogebra applets

Step 1: Open geogebra app in your system.

Step 2: In the input bar type the function $\frac{x^2}{a^2} - \frac{y^2}{b^2} = 1$

Step 3: Then type P =point(eq1) where eq1 is the function name obtained in step 2

Step 4: Again, type the equation $\frac{x^2}{2} - \frac{y^2}{2} = 0$

Step 5: Next type $V1 = (-a, 0)$

Step 6: $V2 = (a, 0)$

Step 7: $F1 = (-\sqrt{(a^2 + b^2)}, 0)$

Step 8: $F2 = (\sqrt{(a^2 + b^2)}, 0)$

Step 9: Then we go to the tool bar, click on segment and join the pints P to $F1$ and P to $F2$

Step 10: Right click on the segment $PF1$ and go to setting then goto show label change name to value and closed it.

Step 11: Click on play button in step 3 in input bar to see that $PF1 + PF2 = constant$

5.4.2 Observations

(i) The graph of $\frac{x^2}{a^2} - \frac{y^2}{b^2} = 1$ forms a hyperbola.

(ii) If $a < b$ the curve of hyperbola decreases but when $a = 0$ the hyperbola disappears.

(iii) If $a < b$ the curve of hyperbola increases but when $b = 0$ the hyperbola disappear.

(iv) When $a = b = 0$ the graph disappear.

5.4.3 Conclusion

Hence we traced the hyperbola in cartesian coordinate as shown in figure5.4.

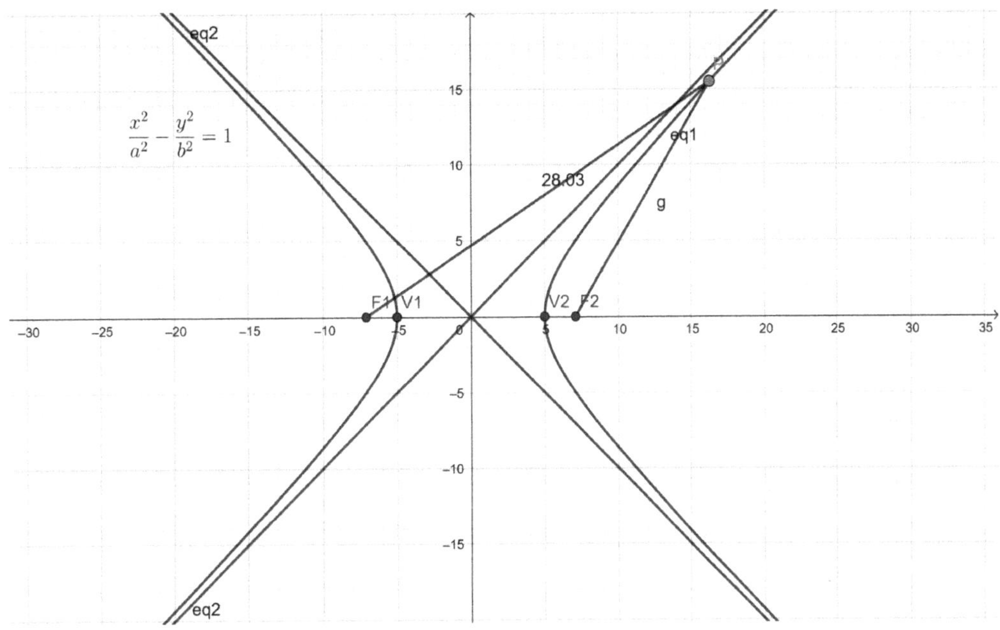

Figure 5.4: Hyperbola in cartesian coordinates

5.5 Tracing of circle in polar coordinate about the initial line

System requirement:- (i) Windows OS or Android Phone

(ii) Geogebra software

Prerequisite:

(i) Geogebra interface: How to use geogebra

(ii) Knowledge of circle in polar coordinates.

Equation of circle in polar coordinates is $r = 2a\cos\theta$

Which is circle with radius a passing through pole and having diameter through

pole as initial line.

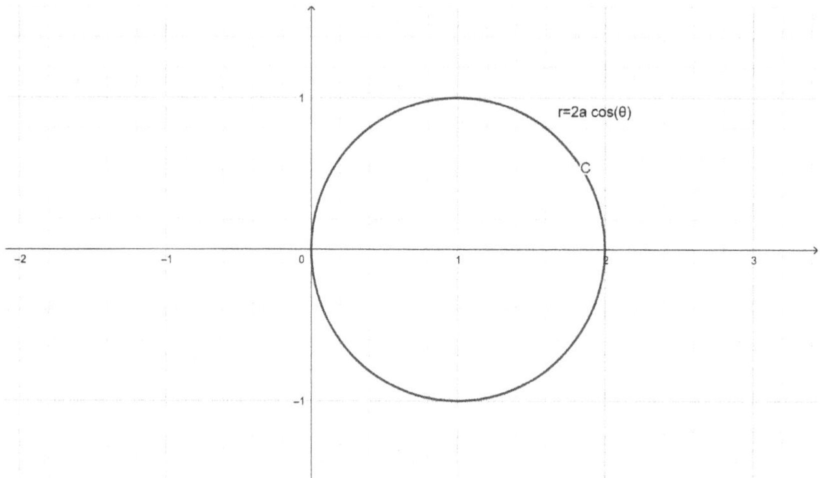

Figure 5.5: Circle in polar coordinate

5.5.1 Procedure or Geogebra Applets

Step 1: Open the geogebra app in your system.

Step 2: In the input bar type $a = 1$

Step 3: Type the function $r = 2a \cos\theta$ in the input bar.

5.5.2 Observations

(i) As a increases, the size of the circle increases in the positive x-axes and as a decreases the size of the circle again increases but in the negative x-axes.

(ii) The curve passes through pole at $\theta = \frac{\pi}{2}$

5.5.3 Conclusion

The curve formed is a circle as shown in figure 5.5.

5.6　To trace cardioid in polar coordinate

System requirement: (i) Windows OS and android phone

(ii) Geogebra Classic 6

Pre requisite:

(i) Geogebra interface

(ii) Knowledge of cardioid

A cardioid is a plane curve trace by a point on the perimeter of circle that is ruling around a fix circle of a same radius.

In the polar coordinate system the equation of cardioid is given by

$r = a(1 + cos(\theta))$

5.6.1　Procedure or geogebra applets

Step 1: Open geogebra app in your system.

Step 2: Type $a = 1$ in the input bar sliders with default value varies from -5 to 5 will come.

Step 3: Type the function $r = a(1 + cos(\theta))$

Step 4: In the input bar type $P = point(b)$

Step 5: Again add equation $O = (0, 0)$

Step 6: By changing the value of a it show the figure changing it size but by changing the value of r figure doesnot changes.

Step 7: Go to input bar then click on segment and select point P and O to make a segment and then click on move button to see the effect.

5.6.2　Observations

(i) The diagram of function $r = a(1 + cos(\theta))$ form a heart shape curve.

(ii) When the value of a increases the curve increases.

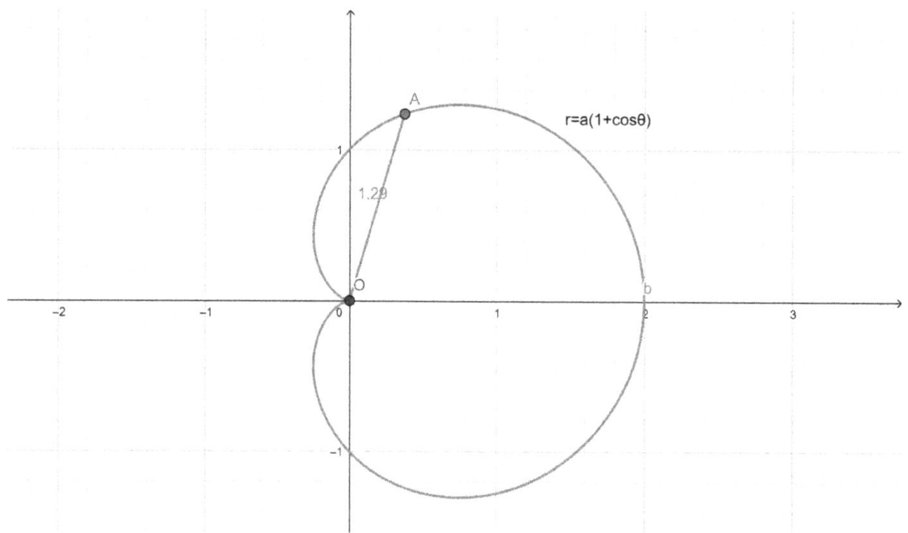

Figure 5.6: Cardiod in polar coordinate

5.6.3 Conclusion

The graph of the cardioid is obtained as shown in figure 5.6

5.7 Tracing of lemniscate in polar coordinate

System requirement:- (i) Windows OS or Android Phone

(ii) Geogebra software

Prerequisite:

(i) Geogebra interface: How to use geogebra

(ii) Knowledge about lemniscate in polar coordinates.

Lemniscate: Equation of lemniscate is $r^2 = a^2 \cos \theta$.

A lemniscate is symmetrical about initial line and radius vector. Tangents to the curve are $\theta = \pm \frac{\pi}{4}$. It has two loops symmetrical about initial line and r-axes.

5.7.1 Procedure or Geogebra applets

Step 1: Open geogebra app in your system.

Step 2: In the input bar, type $a = 1$ slider with default value -5 to 5 will come

Step 3: Type $g(x) = -x$ and $f(t) = t$

Step 4: Then go to ABC text in tool bar and click on the line $g(x)$ in the graph and type $\theta = -\frac{-\pi}{4}$ and then click on the line $f(x)$ in the graph and type $\theta = -\frac{-\pi}{4}$

Note: ABC text bar is not available in geogebra classic 5 software you can skip this step there.

Step 5: Type $\text{Curve}(a\sqrt{\cos(2\theta)}, \theta, 0, 2\pi)$ in the input bar

5.7.2 Observations

(i) Lemniscate curve form nodes at the pole.

(ii) The curve is symmetrical about both r and θ

(iii) The curve passes through pole.

(iv) The tangent to the curve are $\theta = \frac{-\pi}{4} \, \& \, \frac{\pi}{4}$

5.7.3 Conclusion

The graph of lemniscate is obtained as shown in figure 5.7. The length of nodes increases as a increases and disappears at $a = 0$.

5.8 Tracing of rose curve in polar coordinate

System requirement:- (i) Windows OS or Android Phone

(ii) Geogebra software

Prerequisite:

(i) Geogebra interface: How to use geogebra

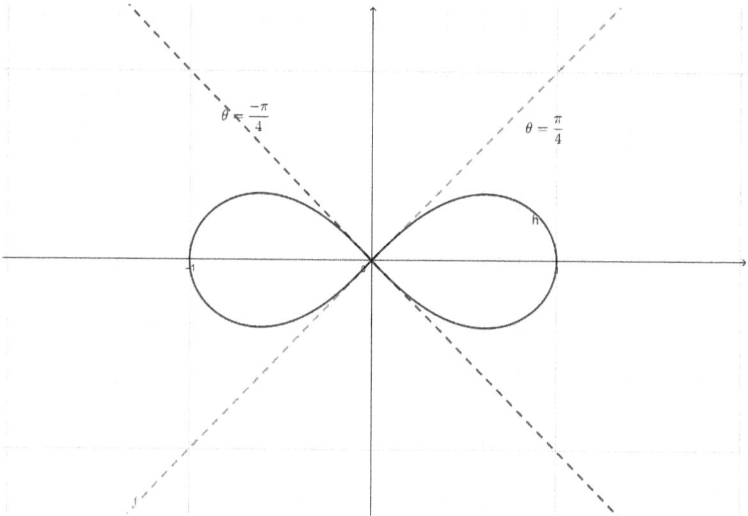

Figure 5.7: Lemniscate in polar coordinate

(ii) Knowledge about rose curve & polar coordinates.

Equation of rose curve is $r = a \cos n\theta$

This curve is named as rose because graph of the function appears as petals of rose flower.

5.8.1 Procedure or geogebra applets

Step 1: Open geogebra app in your system.

Step 2: In the input bar, type $n = 4$ a slider with default value -5 to 5 will come. Change the default value to 2 to any number say 10.

Step 3: Type $a = 1$

Step 4: Type the function $r = a \cos n\theta$

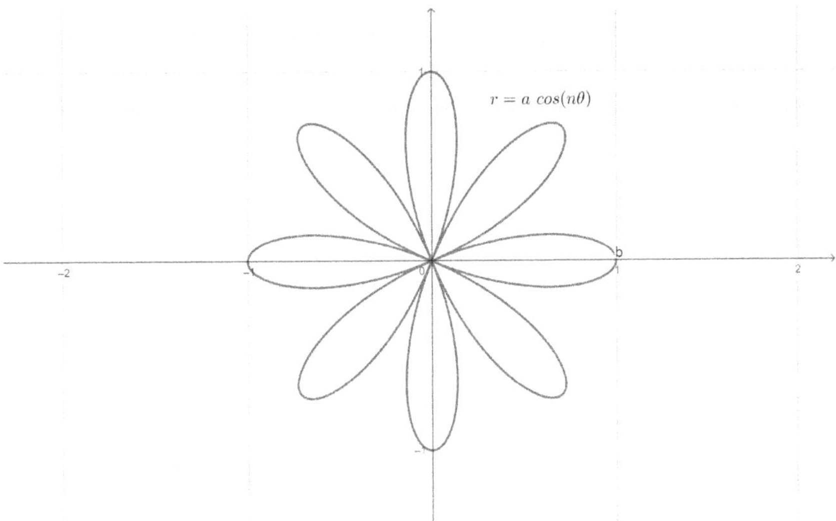

Figure 5.8: Rose curve in polar coordinate

5.8.2   Observations

(i) Nmber of petals depends on the value n i.e. If n is even, then number of petals in the graph are $2n$ and if n is odd then number of petals in the graph are n.

(ii) The graph disappears at $a = 0$.

(iv) For $n = 0$ the curve is circle with center at origin, for $n = 1$ the curve is circle which touch the origin, for $n \geq 2$ the curve form petals

5.8.3   Conclusion

Rose curve is a perdiodic function. It is an even function. The petals are symmetrical about the initial line. The graph of function is as shown in figure 5.8

Chapter 6

Sketching 3D Graphs

In this chapter we will discuss sketching of ellipsoid, hyperboloid of one and two sheets, elliptic cone, elliptic paraboloid, hyperboloid paraboloid using cartesian coordinates.

6.1 Graph of ellipsoid in cartesian coordinate

System requirement: Windows OS and Geogebra Classic 6

Pre requisite:

(i) Geogebra interface

(ii) Knowledge of a ellipse and elliposoid.

Ellipsoid: Equation of ellipse

$$\frac{x^2}{a^2} + \frac{y^2}{b^2} = 1$$

Elliposoid is the $3D$ presentation of ellipse. It has three independent axis and usually specified by the length a, b, c of the three semi axes.

Equation of ellipsoid

$$\frac{x^2}{a^2} + \frac{y^2}{b^2} + \frac{z^2}{c^2} = 1$$

6.1.1 Procedure or geogebra applets

Step 1: Open geogebra app in your system.

Step 2: Next open the 3D calculator

Step 3: In the input bar, type $a = 1$, $b = 1$, $c = 1$, slider for a, b, c with default value from -5 to 5 will come.

Step 4: Type the function $\frac{x^2}{a^2} + \frac{y^2}{b^2} + \frac{z^2}{c^2} = 1$

Step 5: By changing the position of a, b and c in the slides we can see the effect on the graph.

6.1.2 Observations

(i) The graph of the function $\frac{x^2}{a^2} + \frac{y^2}{b^2} + \frac{z^2}{c^2} = 1$ form an elliposoid.

(ii) When $a < b \,\&\, a < c$; $b < a \,\&\, b < c$; $c < a \,\&\, c < b$ sphere expand its size and forms into an oval shape.

(iii) When any of slides a, b, c is 0 the sphere disappear.

(iv) If $a = b = c = 0$ the ellipse disappear

(v) If $a = b = c = 1$ the ellipsoid is a sphere.

6.1.3 Conclusion

The graph of the elliposoid obtained as shown in figure 6.1.

6.2 Graph of hyperboloid of one and two sheets in cartesian coordinate

System requirement: Windows OS and Geogebra Classic 6

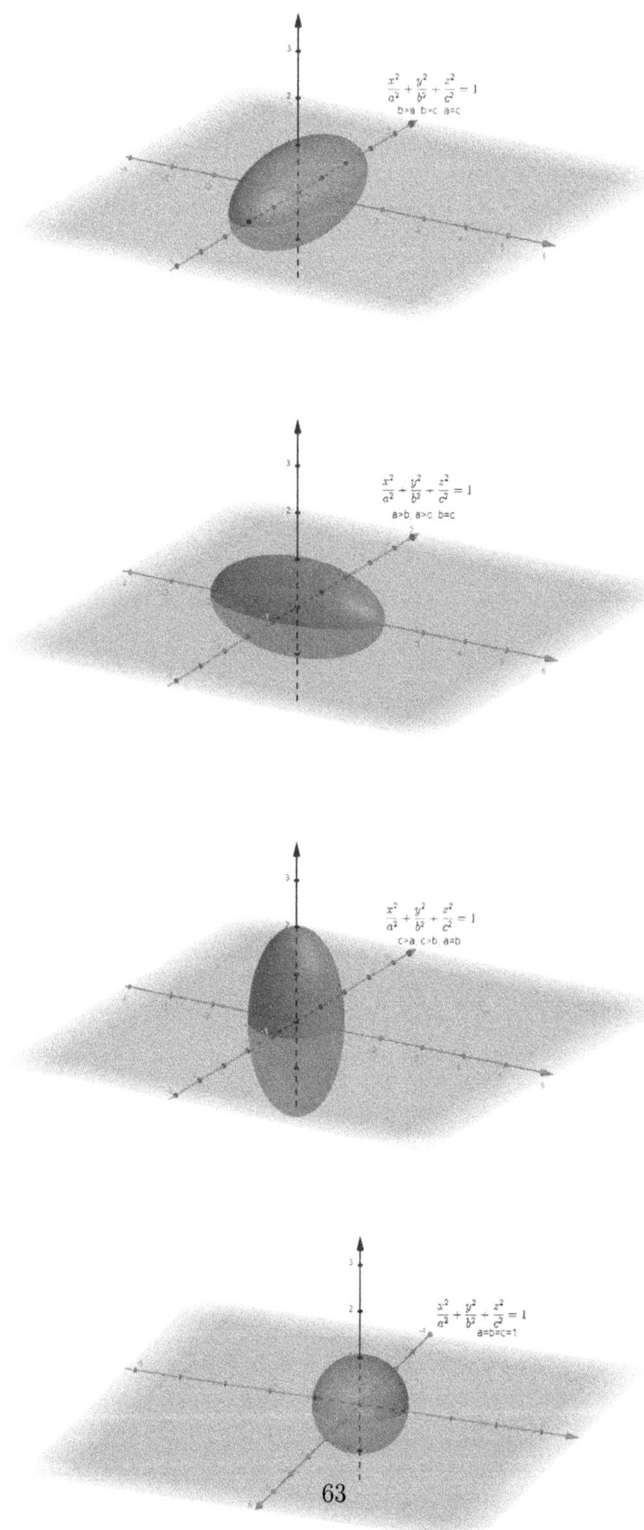

Figure 6.1: Elliposoid in cartesian coordinate

Pre requisite:

(i) Geogebra interface

(ii) Knowledge of hyperboloid.

Hyperboloid: A hyperboloid is a quadratic surface which may be one or two sheeted.

Hyperboloid of one sheet: The one-sheeted hyperboloid is a surface of revolution obtained by rotating a hyperbola about the perpendicular bisector to the line between the foci.

The equation of one sheeted hyperboloid is $\frac{x^2}{a^2} + \frac{y^2}{b^2} - \frac{z^2}{c^2} = 1$

Hyperboloid of two sheets: The equation of one sheeted hyperboloid is $\frac{Z^2}{c^2} - \frac{x^2}{b^2} - \frac{y^2}{c^2} = 1.$

6.2.1 Procedure or geogebra applets

Step 1: Open 3D calculator in geogebra app in your system.

Step 2: In the input bar we type $a = b = c = 1$ then the slider for a, b and c will come. The default values of a, b, c varies from -5 to 5.

Step 3: Next type the function hyperboloid of one sheet i.e. $\frac{x^2}{a^2} + \frac{y^2}{b^2} - \frac{z^2}{c^2} = 1$ and hyperboloid of two sheets i.e. $\frac{Z^2}{c^2} - \frac{x^2}{b^2} - \frac{y^2}{c^2} = 1.$

Step 4: By changing the position of a, b and c in the slider we can see the effect of a, b and c on the graph.

6.2.2 Observations:

The graph of the function of the hyperboloid of one sheet i.e. $\frac{x^2}{a^2} + \frac{y^2}{b^2} - \frac{z^2}{c^2} = 1$ form two connected cones and the graph of hyperboloid of two sheets i.e. $\frac{z^2}{c^2} - \frac{x^2}{b^2} - \frac{y^2}{c^2} = 1$ forms two disconnected cones.

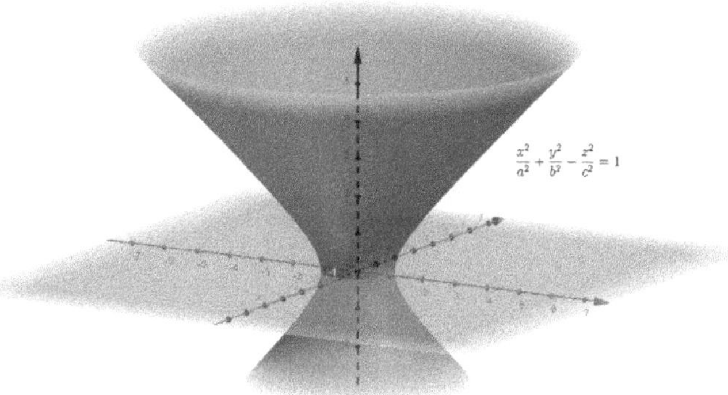

Figure 6.2: Hyperboloid of one sheet

6.2.3   Conclusion

The graph of hyperboloid of one sheet and hyperboloid of two sheets is as shown in figure6.2 and 6.3

6.3   Graph elliptic cone in cartesian coordinate

System requirement: Windows OS and Geogebra Classic 6

Pre requisite:

(i) Geogebra interface

(ii) Knowledge of elliptic cone.

Elliptic cone: A cone is a three dimensional geometric shape created by connecting the points on a circular base to a common point known as the apex or vertex using a series of line segments or lines.

Standard Equation of Elliptic Cone:

$$\frac{(x - x_\circ)^2}{a^2} + \frac{(y - y_\circ)^2}{b^2} = \frac{(z - z_\circ)^2}{c^2}$$

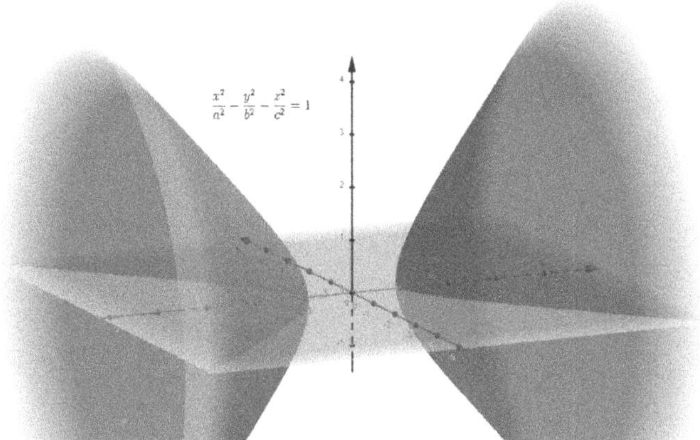

Figure 6.3: Hyperboloid of two sheets

6.3.1   Procedure or geogebra applets

Step 1: Open 3D calculator in geogebra app in your system

Step 2: In the input bar we type $a = b = c = 1$, then the slider for a, b, &, c will be appear in input bar. The value of a, b, &, c varies from -5 to 5.

Step 3: Next type the function $\frac{(x-x_\circ)^2}{a^2} + \frac{(y-y_\circ)^2}{b^2} = \frac{(z-z_\circ)^2}{c^2}$.

Step 4: By changing the position of a, b, &c in the slider we can see the effect of a, b, &c on the graph.

6.3.2   Observations

(i) All three variables with degree two terms present.

(ii) Two variable of degree two are positive and one is negative when equation equals 0.

(iii) Axes is parallel to negative variable.

(iv) Two cones with common vertex is obtained.

6.3.3   Conclusion

The graph of elliptic conic is as shown in figure6.4

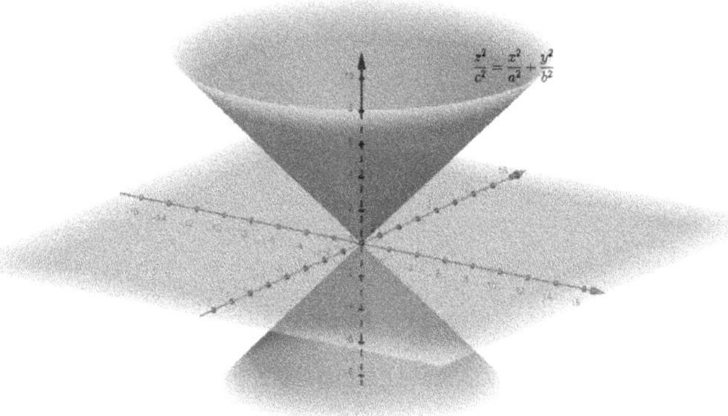

Figure 6.4: Elliptic cone in cartesian coordinate

6.4 Graph of elliptic paraboloid in cartesian coordinate

System requirement: (i) Windows OS and android phone

(ii) Geogebra Classic 6

Pre requisite:

(i) Geogebra interface

(ii) Knowledge of elliptic paraboloid.

A paraboloid that can be put into a position such that it section parallel to one coordinate plane are elllipse while its section parallel to other two coordinate planes are parabolas. Equation of elliptic paraboliod is

$$\frac{z}{c} = \frac{x^2}{a^2} + \frac{y^2}{b^2}$$

6.4.1 Procedure or geogebra applets

Step 1: Open geogebra 3D calculator app in your system.

Step 2: Type $a = 1, b = 1, c = 1$ in the input bar, where a, b, c varies from -5 to 5

Step 3: Next we type function $\frac{z}{c} = \frac{x^2}{a^2} + \frac{y^2}{b^2}$

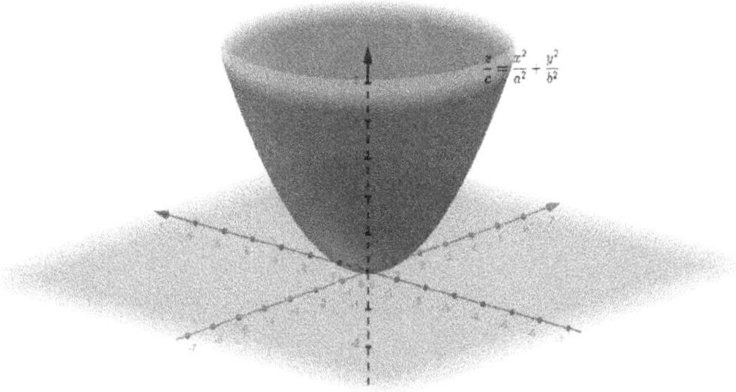

Figure 6.5: Elliptic paraboloid in cartesian coordinate

Step 4: By changing the position of $a, b \, \& c$ in the slider we can see the changes in graph.

6.4.2 Observations

(i) The graph of the elliptic paraboliod

$$\frac{z}{c} = \frac{x^2}{a^2} + \frac{y^2}{b^2}$$

is open upward when $c > 0$ and downward when $c < 0$.

(ii) Horizontal trace is ellipse

(iii) Vertical trace is parabola

6.4.3 Conclusion

We trace the graph of the elliptic paraboloid in cartesian coordinate as shown in figure 6.5.

6.5 Graph of hyperboloid paraboloid in cartesian coordinate

System requirement: Windows OS and Geogebra Classic 6

Pre requisite:

(i) Geogebra interface

(ii) Knowledge of hyperboloid paraboloid.

A hyperbolic paraboloid is a doubly curved surface that resemble the shape of a saddle, it has a convex form along one axes and a concave form along other axes

Equation of hyperbolic paraboloid is

$$\frac{z}{c} = \frac{x^2}{a^2} - \frac{y^2}{b^2}$$

6.5.1 Procedure or geogebra applets

Step 1: Open the geogebra app

Step 2: Click on 3D calculator.

Step 3: Type $a = 1$, $b = 1$, $c = 1$ in the input bar sliders for $a, b \,\& c$ will come with default value from -5 to 5.

Step 4: Next, we type the function $\frac{z}{c} = \frac{x^2}{a^2} - \frac{y^2}{b^2}$.

Step 5: By changing the value of a, b, $\& c$ we can see the change in the diagram.

6.5.2 Observations

(i) The graph of the curve $\frac{z}{c} = \frac{x^2}{a^2} - \frac{y^2}{b^2}$ form a doubly curve surface like saddle.

(ii) Horizontal traces are ellipse

(iii) Vertical traces are parabolas

6.5.3 Conclusion

We trace the graph of the hyperboliod paraboloid in cartesian coordinate as shown in figure 6.6.

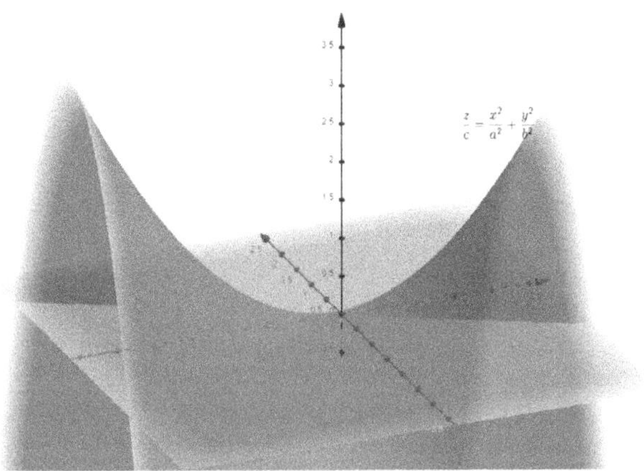

Figure 6.6: Hyperbolic paraboloid in cartesian coordinate

How to Install Geogebra and Use it

Download Geogebra Windows installer from google (for android phone download from the play store one can also used geogebra from web browser without installing it in your system) and double click to open the file then follow instruction given by browser and complete the installation.

How to save files in geogebra:

Click on the bar
Goto save
Signin
Save the files in .ggb extension for future use

How to open files in geogebra:

Click on bar
Click on Open
Signin
Double click on the file to be open.

How to import graphics in MS word and Latex

Click in DownloadAS (sometime it is found in export image)
Click on PNG or PDF document
Click on export.

MS word
Impart as ordinary pictures in MS word
Latex
Use command $includegraphics[scale = ...]FileName$